MW00625189

LAURA SIMON

Did She Say That Out Loud?

By Laura Simon

Represented by AuthorizeMe Literary Firm,
Sharon Norris Elliott, Agent
PO BOX 1816, South Gate, CA 90280,
www.AuthorizeMe.net   AuthorizeMeNow@gmail.com

All Scripture references from The Message, © 2002,
Eugene H. Peterson, unless otherwise noted

ISBN: 978-1-956654-74-5

Endorsements

Laura Simon's "tell it like it is" personality shines through every page. *Did She Say That Out Loud?* takes you behind the scenes and then to center stage by asking thought provoking questions. This is a must read not just for PWs but for anyone in leadership.

~*Cledra Gross, Equipped for Destiny Church, Author, Life Coach, Entrepreneur, South Carolina*

I thank Laura Simon for writing this book, *Did She Say That Out Loud?* It's wonderful! I love it! The book is much needed. All week, I see it with my clients, and I know it will be a tremendous help for pastors, pastor's wives, and people in leadership. The honest dialogue about the feelings in the fishbowl life make it an important read, and I'm glad Laura Simon put it out into the world.

~*Rev. Dr. Jacqueline Harris, Psychologist, Professor, Pastor's Wife, First Baptist Church of Glenn Valley, Riverside, California*

I think Laura Simon's *Did She Say That Out Loud?* is hilarious!!!!! Keep it as it is!!!!! I love it and think it would be a tremendous asset to the Pastor and Pastor's Wife's Library. Request to Lady Laura: I would like Idris Elba to play me in the movie. The book humorously shows how we grew together in ministry and learned the tricks of the trade for ministry during the 2020 Pandemic Season. *Did She Say That Out Loud?* gives the reader a ringside seat into our Fishbowl Life. Author-1st-Lady Laura Simon is genuine. I always know where I stand with Truth-Tellers Pastor Tony & 1st Lady Laura. Great truth-telling read that absolutely solidifies our Lil-Big-Sister-Lil-Brother relationship.

~ Rev. Robert Harris, Senior Pastor, First Baptist Church of Glenn Valley, Riverside; Business Owner, Lake Elsinore, California

What an amazing eye-opener and much needed guide Laura Simon's *Did She Say That Out Loud?* is! This book shows us how God can work in any situation; especially those that take us through every emotion! This book is necessary in times like these!

~Lady Donna Sneed, Bethesda Community Church, Author, Designer, Entrepreneur, Albany, Georgia

Laura Simon has created a book that will help Pastor's Wives and those in leadership handle the many different obstacles with a great attitude and reminding us to extend grace and mercy. Did She Say That Out Loud? reminds us that it's okay to have new things, and we don't have to shy away from God's blessings to us. Laura also reminds us to simply keep it real! I am grateful Did She Say That Out Loud? is a book that speaks straight to the heart.

~Chantelle D. Sylvester, Pastor's Wife, Teacher, St Mary Missionary Baptist Church, Port Barre, Louisiana

As a Pastor's Wife, Mom, and Business professional, *Did She Say That Out Loud?* kept me on the edge of my seat! This body of work exudes humor, relatability, and transparency. Women from all walks of life will connect with the author's organic and real-world communication style.

~*Lady Ashlee Buckley, MBA, Voices of Faith, Baton Rouge, Louisiana*

"Why come they can say what they want and I can't?" is one of my favorite questions posed in Laura Simon's *Did She Say That Out Loud?* She writes about knowing your role, being anointed for the pastor's wife position, and understanding that you never want to embarrass God. I love how she shared the change in her attitude after several humbling encounters with God. Did She Say That Out Loud? impresses upon us to stay humble, and God will fight "those" battles. ~*Rev. Jackie M. Baker, Pasadena, Texas*

Laura Simon's *Did She Say That Out Loud?* is a must-read that clearly shows how often we can be judgmental. The stories shared reminded my husband and I about certain experiences we have encountered while trying to break the church dress code. We understood Laura's heart regarding how traditional dress can kill a church from saving the lost. *Did She Say That Out Loud?* keeps pointing the reader back to Romans 12:1-2 and 1 Thessalonians 5:14-15, which reminds all of us to be transformed so we can see the best in others, accept the fact we're all different, and make sure we bring out the best in everyone, so we are not so concerned with what people are wearing. I'm sure this book will be a tremendous help to others.

~*Pastor Michael Neal, Sr., & Evangelist Maritza Neal, Iron Sharpens Iron Ministries, Prayer Ministry &*

Children's Ministry Leader, Tustin, California

I absolutely loved the story Laura Simon shared in Chapter 11 of *Did She Say That Out Loud?* for so many reasons. As a pastor's wife, I think we can all relate to having a Miss Sally in the congregation. Readers will find themselves seeing the interactions of the characters like Miss Sally and Ron, along with Laura. Her phone conversation was so real. Loved, loved, loved it all!
~Dr. Alisa Carter, Pastor's Wife, Business Owner, King's Bible Church, Grand Rapids, Michigan

Did She Say That Out Loud? by Laura Simon is a MUST READ. I wish I'd read this before starting ministry alongside my pastor-husband in October 1993. I Quit was both hilarious and serious. How can that be? The answer is simple: Author Laura Simon. Did She Say That Out Loud? is an easy read. It will make you laugh and cry. It should be a prerequisite for all pastors. I tilt my First Lady's Hat to Lady Laura.
~Lena Like, Pastor's Widow since 11-1-2021, God's Grace Church, St. Louis, Missouri

Laura Simon's Did She Say That Out Loud? has a chapter that is the most honest and transparent sharing of the challenges of dressing as a PW in the African American Culture I have read! I also love how she shared the process of her growth and how she has walked it out. The best part is how she has mentored other PW's on the same journey!
~Jacqi Bell Henry, Pastor's Wife, Macedonia Missionary Baptist Church, Wilmington, North Carolina

"Did She Say That Out Loud?" is a phenomenal book! ALLLLL of the chapter titles had me eager to dive in! Laura Simon shares openly and truthfully about her experiences in ministry - experiences that many of us can relate to as pastors' wives but may be afraid to speak about out loud. The struggle is real! Laura Simon welcomes and encourages all who desire to lead with honesty, transparency, and a sense of humor.

~Evelyn Wilson Kay, First Lady, Teacher, First Baptist Church North Brentwood, Maryland

How Fake Do You Want Me To Be? is a chapter in the new book Did She Say That Out Loud? by Laura Simon that was meant for me. It's like the words were screaming out to me. I serve on the local mental health board, and in ministry as a pastor's wife, and any woman who wants to remain authentic and remember their identity needs to read this book. It's as real as it gets. Kudos to Laura Simon!

~Lady LaVonne Ward, Mental Health Counselor, Ministry Leader, Second Baptist Church, Lima, Ohio

Did She Say That Out Loud? is a thought provoking, insightful commentary on how being able to share one's vulnerability and self-truth are key to being able to live and experience the full measure of who God intended you to be. Laura Simon shares her truths, and ministry life experiences, and stresses although we are weak, He is strong!

~Chanel McCoy, Mother, Women's Ministry, Business Owner, Calvary Church, Tustin, California

I love it! Laura Simon's *Did She Say That Out*

Loud? did an amazing job of being transparent, while wonderfully capturing the audience's attention with stories people can relate to in more ways than one. Throughout the book, I felt like I could relate, and I *understood* her feelings. Laura Simon allows the reader to share in her feelings and take a walk alongside her while she navigates her ministry life. I *understood* her feelings. *Did She Say That Out Loud?* takes people to a place where they can see themselves.

~Juanita Phillips, Women's Ministry, Praise Leader, New Covenant Church, Long Beach, California

Laura Simon has written a must read in *Did She Say That Out Loud?* More specifically, Chapter 7 – Don't Help Me, I Hate the Village. Laura's book spoke to me in a very personal way. To this day, I have regrets about not allowing my one, and only daughter to spend the night with friends and some family. However, after reading Chapter 7, I realize I made a wise decision. *Did She Say That Out Loud?* has given me a new perspective on church folks and the like thereof. It's a great read and hilarious I might add.

~Ingris Clark, Minister, Women's Ministry, Hemet, California

Laura Simon's Converted: But You Can Still Catch These Hands in her new book, *Did She Say That Out Loud?* is intriguing, relatable, and funny. Great storytelling that includes down to earth experiences. Enjoyed how it ties back to the relationship with God, how you walk and talk with him, as well as the thought provoking questions that promote reflection at the end.

~Leonna Cannon, Mother of two, Millennial,

Women's Ministry, Starlight Baptist Church, Santa Ana, California

Did She Say That Out Loud? is a book that speaks to Everyone. Women in ministry as well as women in the general all deal with the same issues regarding husbands, children, working, stay-at-home, and being a friend. Reading this will help all. The book even can help men to understand what women go through. *Did She Say That Out Loud?* shows the struggle of a woman that loves God, wants Him to be pleased with her, and wants to make Him smile. I am sure everyone will relate.

~Sonya Tabb, Women's Ministry Leader, Entrepreneur, Menifee, California

Laura Simon keeps it real, raw, and relevant in her new book, *Did She Say That Out Loud?* This book is thoughtful, provoking, and mindful, while helping the reader to remember to be prayerful, trust God, and to remove the masks that hide who we really are or want to be. Own up when you're wrong is a theme woven throughout, while encouraging the reader to see the best in others like Jesus.

~Gwendolyn Richardson, Praise & Worship Leader, Women's Ministry, Business Owner, GMR Enterprise, Brea, California

Laura Simon's *Did She Say That Out Loud?* is captivating and takes readers on a personal journey into her life as a Pastor's Wife working to be transparent in doing ministry with her pastor husband, yet vulnerable with the fellow Church Members. Laura allows us to share in her life through humorous stories and thought-provoking questions that make the reader take a look at themselves. I loved it!

~Evelyn Jackson, Worship Ministry, Business Owner, Covenant Fellowship, Orange, California

The book, "Did She Say That Out Loud?" is a frank and open look into the life of a pastor's wife with valuable takeaways. Who knew you could learn, "what you treasure may be my junk" and "get along among yourselves, be patient with each other" in one chapter? Such insights are within all the chapters, which makes this book a "must read". I like the fact that the book encourages the readers to participate with its questions and motivational prayers at the end of each chapter.

~Joan Wilkinson, Children's Ministry Leader, Women's Ministry Group Leader, St. James-Covenant City Ministries, Anaheim, California

Laura Simon will take you from laughter to deep thought over and over again. In her new book, *Did She Say That Out Loud?* Laura weaves the details of her experiences in a way that will have you hanging on to every word. You'll be shocked and challenged. This book is a must read.

~Lady Susan Damon, Wife of Pastor Juan Damon, Mother, Friend; Alabama, Connecticut, Northeastern Conference of Seventh-day Adventists

DID SHE SAY THAT OUT LOUD?

Acknowledgments

My heartfelt love and appreciation go to my PastorMan-Hubby Tony Simon, who has been my greatest supporter since I told him about writing this book in 2008, to now, when he continually pushed me to keep writing and hurry up and finish it. Much gratitude also goes to Tony Simon for going with me in 2009, setting up a booth, and helping me sell my homemade books at Dr. Lois Evans' Pastor's Wives Conference in Dallas, Texas, which was the precursor to *Did She Say That Out Loud?* Thanks, Babe.

A ginormous thank you goes to my cheerleading color coordinating daughters, Kennedy and Sydni, who made sure the book cover was colorful, eye catching, not boring, and appealed to them. Another great big thank you to my sons, Sagel2 and Jonathan, the greatest hype-men a mom could ever ask for. They're the team that made sure, at least twice a month to tell me just how famous I was going to be once the book hit the market. They have so much confidence in me and I'm so grateful. Anytime and every time Jonathan noticed discouragement in me, he'd remind me that he was the first child to tell me I was going to be a famous writer back in 2018! And Sagel2's claim to fame for me started in 2019, just a smidgen after J. For that, I am forever thankful. Their belief in me and my writing abilities is beyond what I could ever dream or imagine. I love you all, my four Children of the Corn.

To my parents, Johnny and Rosette Williams who keep me striving for that best seller status. Also, so grateful and thankful for parents that keep me humble, and on my face before the Lord. They make sure I don't ever get beside myself. Ha! Fame? Just finish the book already so we can see what's going to happen next.

And crazy-forever-grateful-gratitude to my nephew, son, little brother, former boss, church member, pizza-guy-want-a-slice? (*only* he knows what that's about) friend, and JFK Transportation, Incorporated, Kappa Man, Kevin Watson. He's been my guy, my dude, my YOU CAN DO IT Laura Simon since forever. He has been the best believer in me, the best supporter of me, and the best behind-the-scenes-tell-me-what-you-need-so-we-can-make-it-happen-otherwise-there-wouldn't-be-a-book, *Did She Say That Out Loud?* and I'll write you a card of encouragement but you better not open it until you're away from me, and you better not cry when you open it up and read it. Next to Tony Simon, he's the man. Thank you, Kevin Curtis Carter Watson (my name for him that I got from his mom, Mrs. Phyllis Watson). Big shout out to Miss Phyllis! She and Mr. Floyd were two of our biggest supporters when Tony was a new pastor, and I was a new pastor's wife.

To my family, church family and church friends,

and to all that helped encourage me throughout the Live Late Night Lattes, Laughter & Life with Lady Laura journey and continue to help build my platform, thank you! It wouldn't be what it is without you!

To my Pastor's Wives' Posse PWDW: Y'all are the best support group a PW could ask for! Rain or shine, you ladies ALWAYS come through for me. Learning to navigate the 2020 Fishbowl Life was far less painful because of you. I love and appreciate you more than you'll ever know. Thank you DFW Pastors' Wives for making me an honorary part of the Texas Sisterhood, even though I'm a CaliGirl.

My Line Sisters, My Sorority Sisters of Alpha Kappa Alpha Sorority, Incorporated who share my content, come on, come in, and stop by whenever they see me in need of support; just know I see you, and appreciate your love, encouragement, and all things that make me smile.

And, lastly, but not because she's not important, is my Agent, the one and only, Sharon Norris Elliott. Thank you for believing in me and signing me as your Number Two Daughter-Client-Problem-Child. My words cannot express how grateful I am, and appreciative of your continued support and all the things you've taught me, how you've made sure I can stand strong and tall in any writing arena, how you have made sure I have the best tools, the best resources, and if I don't have it at first, you make sure certain I get it later. Thank you for praying over me and petitioning God on my behalf for my writing ministry, because it's more than a writing career. I appreciate you for inviting me into the Sisterhood of Christian Writers who love Jesus and love you. I'm absolutely giddy with excitement to see what the Father is going to do through you next. The best is yet to come.

Dedication

To Tony
Thank you for being the little boy
who loved me 51 years ago in the first grade.

~

To Clyde & Saunja
You are our friends.
Thank you for taking the journey with us.
Together, Together

~

He told me to write the book
And share the stories,
Because his wife, Almie, and others needed it.
For you,
Carey Latimore

~

Laura Simon

LAURA SIMON

Table of Contents

LAURA SIMON

.

Chapter 1
In The Beginning

The comedians I love most are the ones who allow me to look into the face of humanity and laugh until I cry and my stomach hurts. Then they follow the side-splitting tales with the phrase, "I can't make this stuff up!"

Such is the reality of my life as a pastor's wife. Little did I know that my husband's installation would thrust me into what seems like a stand-up career every time I open my mouth to talk about my existence. Just like church members see the parsonage as their personal common gathering area, they often see the pastor's wife as some sort of breathing journal. They can write anything in it that comes to mind with no thought of the emotional feelings of the page. I'm that living page, y'all.

But the book you hold in your hands is not really about what other people write on my page. It's not a book that's trying to straighten out the crazy people in the congregation. This book tells the stories of my experiences—and yes, of many pastors' wives who just can't bring themselves to share as openly—to reveal and heal the tender heart of the woman in this unique role. All the cliches are true—I have to laugh to keep from crying, and I can't make this stuff up. No matter what, though, God has specific answers for how He wants us to act and react in our position both as individual Christians and as the woman who stands at her husband's side.

Did you know what you were getting into when you became a pastor's wife? Like really, did you have any idea what you were in for?

Yeah. Me either. Girl, please. Let's just be honest and say it. No, I had no idea what I was in for. Am I talking to you from this page? Yes, I can almost hear you. Absolutely. As a matter of fact, Sunshine, I am grinning and laughing out loud because I can just about see your face. Literally.

And don't mind me, I'm not laughing *at* you, I'm laughing *with* you. I mean who else understands what you've been through, what you're going through, and what you're about to go through other than another pastor's wife? Yep. Get ready for the ride of your life, Honey, and I'm here to help you navigate this fishbowl pastor's wife life like a Girl Boss. Yes ma'am. I'll be right here with you.

So how did I come to this? *This* meaning how did I become the Sister-Girl-Guru-Friend to pastors' wives? Easy. I got sick of being fake. Okay. That's not the truth. I have never been fake. I was so sick of being the only minister's wife who then became the only pastor's wife who spoke up—in my city, anyway. I felt like I was in Stepford, Connecticut, hanging out with the Stepford Wives. Nobody would tell the truth, even if her life depended on it. There I was, a part of the PW Sisterhood, and all we did was lie to one another—except for me. I was told I shared too much. We were all either going through the same thing, had already been through the same thing, or were about to go through the same thing, but nobody wanted to talk about it. And I would say, "Are y'all for real?" And they would respond, "My husband said...My husband said...Well, my husband said..."

Exaggerated eye roll.

One day sitting in Starbucks with three other PW's I couldn't take it anymore and screamed, "Oh my stars! Can you guys say anything other than 'My husband said!?' Do you have a thought of your own? I mean, I respect my husband, too, but what the hell?"

That ended all my invites to Starbucks.

I became the Real Rebel, and my four hashtags were born: #real #raw #relevant, and eventually after some time, #refined. And The Preachrzyf (The Preacher's Wife) Movement began.

~

I tried to fit in. Really, I did. But even in the first grade I was labelled the brutally honest, fearless leader. My mother toughened me up and scared me with the devil stories, and the Jesus-doesn't-like-little-girls-who-don't-tell-the-truth threat.

When I was just five years old, I was already used to the fact that my mom wasn't the warm and fuzzy type. Don't get me wrong, she wasn't Mommy Dearest, but she wasn't Claire Huxtable either.

One evening, my dad wasn't home from night school, so it was just my mom and me in the house. I had eaten one of the chocolate Moon Pies my dad bought for me and him. My mom was always watching her 123-pound figure and keeping an eye on my not so flat five-year-old stomach. She didn't want me fat. More on that later.

Anyway, when she asked me about eating the Moon Pie, I lied. She told me the devil was going to get me and I'd be in the lake of fire for not telling the truth. I was scared to death because she said it with a straight face and an ever so slight menacing grin. She didn't yell at me or anything, but since she couldn't get me to admit to anything, she told me I had to take a bath and go to bed. That worked for me, offering me an escape from the conversation. I took a bath, brushed my teeth, and put on my nightgown, then I went into my room, which happened to be directly across from my parent's room. My little table with the shiny, silver legs was the perfect place for me to sit at and drink my pretend coffee before I turned in.

Later that night, Dad came home, ate his Moon Pie, and walked to his room. Mom was in their bathroom brushing her teeth, and I was across the hall, tucked into my canopy bed, but I wasn't asleep. When dad turned on his lamp, the light bouncing off the silver legs of my table and chairs looked like flames. I started screaming.

"Daddy, Daddy! The devil is coming to get me!"

Then I heard my dad ask my mom, "What is she talking about? Why is she screaming, Rosette?"

The light still looked like flickering flames to me, and I yelled out again, "Daddy, Daddy, please save me before the devil gets me!"

Again, I heard him say, "Rosette, what is Laura yelling about? Why is she saying that?"

Dad strolled into my room and tried to comfort me.

"The devil is not going to get you."

"Yes, he is. Look at the fire!"

My dad looked where I pointed. "Laura, that's not fire, that's the light from my lamp. That's Daddy's light flickering on the leg of your table and chairs. It's not the devil. Who told you that?"

For a quick second, I thought I didn't want to snitch on my mom, but then again, yes, I did, so I told on her. I said, "Mommy."

My dad yelled out to my mom, "Rosette? Did you tell this girl the devil was going to get her?"

My mom yelled back, "Yes Johnny, I did! She lied about eating a Moon Pie, so I told her she was going to hell and be in the lake of fire with the devil. She needs to quit lying and tell the truth."

My dad retorted, "Well that isn't the way to tell her about the devil or lying. You done scared her to death."

"Good," my mother said. "Bet she won't be lying anymore." And *that* was the beginning of my no-more-lies-no-fake-jake-no-matter-what life.

One more incident at the hands of my parents sealed the deal on my tendency to be a brutal truth-teller.

As long as I can remember, my dad always had two and three jobs, or was working on an advanced degree in education. Because he was always away at night as either the night school principal, tax consultant/preparer, grad student, or church men's group leader/deacon/trustee, my mom said she wasn't having another baby. My dad wanted another baby, and I wanted a baby brother or sister, but Dad didn't stop working, so the addition of a sibling didn't happen.

One night I was home with my dad while my mom and her best friend were at school earning their teaching credentials. My mom was late getting home, and my dad was flaming hot. He and I were posted in the garage with the garage door up, holding hands standing at that line where the driveway meets the edge of the garage.

"Where's your mother?"

"I don't know." Seven-year-old me could feel his aggravation.

Just then, my mom sped around the corner, hurriedly turned into the driveway, and pulled forward into the garage. She hadn't gotten out of the car good when my dad thrust me toward her. "Here, I'm leaving. I'm going to my church meeting."

He was in his car, backing out of the driveway, and turning the corner headed to the church before my mom or I could say goodbye. When his taillights left our eyesight, my mom looked down, squeezed my hand, and looked me right in the eyes. "And this is why you will be an only child." How much more brutally honest could someone be? I would be a truth-telling-no-matter-what-the-cost person like my mom from then on.

I hear you. *You mean to tell me you quit lying at the age of seven?* Yes, pretty much. Listen, I told you I'm an only child. Only children usually spend more time with adults than with children their own age. I was an old soul. My babysitter was a Mother in the church with teenage children. My godmother was also a Mother in the church with young adult and teenage children. So, when I was eight, my friends were between 15 and 25. They added to the lessons I was learning about telling the truth.

Hanging out one night with my god-sisters and their boyfriends taught me something about tempering my brutal honesty. One god-sister didn't have a boyfriend. On that night I was the only kid there and I was in on all their adult conversations. Well, I wanted to know why Pat didn't have a man, so I asked her.

"Pat, how come you don't have a boyfriend?"

That question started a fight. "What did you ask me? Who told you to ask me that?"

She got all red in the face and yelled at Lois, "Who told her I didn't have a boyfriend?"

Then she turned on the fellas and said, "Well, who told her to say that?" And everybody just sat there and looked at Pat. "WHO?" she screamed.

With nobody answering her, she was livid, so I finally gathered the courage to say, "Nobody Pat. I just wanted to know, that's all." Her anger, embarrassment, and frustration were combining to cause her to reach her boiling point.

Lois replied again. "No, Pat, nobody told Laura to ask you that. She did it on her own. You know she's grown."

Pat looked at me with this ugly scowl and shrieked, "Don't you ever ask me anything about a man again, do you hear me?"

I looked back at her and said, "Sure Pat. I won't ever ask you about a man again." And I didn't.

What am I trying to say? I've been telling the truth like I see it for over 52 years. God has given me a discerning spirit and I've used the gift since I was a youngster—even though sometimes, obviously, I didn't know how to control it. However, at the tender age of eight I learned to think first, *then* speak.

Plus, when you're an only child, there's no one else to blame for anything. It's either you or *you*. I learned at an early age to tell the truth, so I wouldn't have to remember what I had said. And another thing, my parents pretty much let me speak my mind as long as I spoke my mind in a respectful way. Which I did. They figured, *we know where she stands and what her thought process is on any given subject.* My mom told her sister, "We let the girl say what she wants, because we don't have to worry about her holding it in and trying to kill herself."

I learned it was better just to speak my mind—unless, of course, I was speaking to my god-sister Pat about men.

This truth-telling went on well into middle school, high school, and college. I was always known as the one person who would tell you facts about anything, about any situation, and about yourself. Even I wasn't excluded. My sorority sisters would tell me, "Why don't you just lie? Oh, that's right, you can't." Listen, until they really trained me on how to lie with a straight face and no stuttering (because eventually I did learn the art of lying to boyfriends magnificently), I figured, "Why lie?" I got caught in enough lies as an only child with eagle-eyed-eagle-eared parents that I just said WTH (What the hell?). Yes, that's what I said. My mom always, always, always—did I say always—caught me in my lies. End of story. Eventually, I just stopped lying. It was a waste of time and effort. The saying "It is what it is" could've been made up by me. But it wasn't, although it certainly applies, so here we are.

This all brings us back to this pastors' wives' book. My goal has never been to offend anyone. But I have. (*Long sigh.*) I have been through so much and I've learned so many lessons that I figured I needed to share. If it helps someone not to have to go through any of the stuff I've gone through, I'm telling it. Many pastors' wives have said to me they wish they could say the things I say. Well, since they can't or won't, I will, and I do. No more stomach-aches, headaches, or any other kind of aches from holding it in. No more. And I've also had enough butt taps, ok, "whoopins" from Jesus to know when to speak up with rounded edges and when to completely shut my mouth and stay quiet for those of you who are thinking, "Wow, she really does say everything out loud."

I invite you to look around, peruse the pages, skim the situations, or skip right to the places that speak to your heart or simply pique your interest. Answer the Reflection Questions honestly. Journal or write your thoughts out somewhere. Expression, like confession, is good for the soul.

And let me know what you think. You can reach out if you'd like, and we can have tea and chat. I always love me some tea and I always love me some chat.

~

A Question to Ponder and Laura's Info to Chat

- What would you like to gain from this reading experience?
- Laura Simon Cell ~ 714.400.4183
- Email ~ laurasimonauthor@gmail.com
- Website ~ www.ladylaurasimon.com

PRAYER

Father God, in the Name of Jesus, I ask a special blessing on the sister or brother that's reading this book, the book You ordained me to write, and share. Help them to hear what's in my heart—the words You so lovingly gave to me, even under duress. Please allow Did She Say That Out Loud? to help, and not hinder them or their ministries. Let it be an encouraging word for all their relationships. May it arrest their hearts and convict them where they need to make changes. Let them see through the pages how You've guided me through storms, through mountain top and valley experiences, and how You walked with me and helped me change. Lord, show them You alone can change them, too. Thank You, God for this OH-mazing opportunity to share my life that's been full of lessons that showcase Your love, Your discipline, Your patience, and most of all, Your humor. God I can't wait for everyone to see what an awesome God You are! In Jesus Name.

DID SHE SAY THAT OUT LOUD?

Chapter 2
Who Told You to Wear That?

Who died and made her the pastor-wife-fashion police?"

"Who says I have to dress like her?"

"Why can't I wear what I like – what I want?"

"This is ridiculous. I look ridiculous. I feel ridiculous."

"It's hot. I'm wearing five girdles and Spanx, this suit is shiny and tight, and I feel like a stuffed sausage that landed outside the frying pan."

"I don't think I want to be a pastor's wife anymore." Eye roll. Sigh. Ugh. Does this sound familiar, or is it just me?

My first cousin was a pastor's wife. Her husband was the pastor of a large congregation steeped in tradition. Or rather, *she* was steeped in tradition. She wore the big hats and the long skirts—the super long skirts. She was always in a suit. A shiny suit. And she wore flats or old lady heel shoes.

Each Sunday, they saw her, my kids would ask me, "What is Auntie wearing?" Pause. "She looks like she's wearing a sofa. Mom, she looks like she's wearing upholstery." Upholstery? Who says that? And how, at five, did my kids even know what upholstery was?

I would try to shoosh them, and they'd always come back with, "Who told her to wear that?"

I hated those outfits too, but I was trying to be the good PW, so I would say, "It's pretty!"

And they'd loudly whisper back, "No it's not. She looks like a couch."

When I first became a pastor's wife, I saw all the other PW's and women in leadership wearing those shiny suits, big hats, ugly old-lady height heels, and stockings or pantyhose. I also knew they were stuffed into shapewear—girdles and/or Spanx. And please don't forget the slip. They were wrapped in everything I hated to have to put on. But I was a pastor's wife, so I figured I had to wear that stuff and look the part. I had to look like all the other pastors' wives.

Looking like "them" was a daunting task, but I did it. I had my husband take me to the garment district, the polyester capitol of the world, located in downtown Los Angeles, and home of the Baptist-Church-of-God-in-Christ-Evangelical-Episcapalian-Methodist-Mormon-Pentecostal-You-Name-The-Denomination-of-Your-Choice suits for Church Lady and Church Man. I made my husband—no, no, no, let me rephrase that—I watched my husband lovingly purchase several pricey shiny suits, with big matching hats, and same-material matching shoes. He told me, "Girl, this all looks nice, but don't light a match to these Explode-O Suits. These are not you." The skirts were way too long, but we were determined to have me look like the other wives. We bought into the hype.

On the first Sunday when I wore my first PW get-up, my cousin (the pastor's wife from several paragraphs ago) said I looked sharp. And the other ladies said they were envious. They too said I looked sharp, but they lied. They all lied. The hats, the suits, the shoes: my mother told me the truth.

"Laura, you are 30 years old. That outfit makes you look old, frumpy, and dumpy. You are too short to wear skirts that length—they should be shorter." If anyone was going to tell me the truth, it was my mother. But what was I supposed to do?

Look at these pictures of me at 30 in my PW "costume" and me now, 20 years later. Which looks frumpier? I'll wait.

The truth is: I wore those clothes to impress the other pastor's wives. I didn't wear them for my husband. My husband thought they were over the top, too much, and he hated the fabric. He was not a fan of polyester, and most of those suits were made of that awful flammable material. He bought silk suits for himself. He wanted to buy the same type for me. Problem was, during the early season of our lives and ministry, we just couldn't afford to purchase silk suits for me. I mean, we went shopping once a year at Pastor and Wife Appreciation time. That was the only time we could afford it. My figure was much better suited for form fitting knit suits. But, of course, during the late 90's and early 2000's, those couch, polyester suits were all the rage.

So, who told me to wear those suits? The crowd. My cousin. The other people in my circle. I'm pretty sure those other women held a deep-down reason for telling me I looked great: misery loves company. I found this to be true long after when in the seventh year of our ministry, my husband had an epiphany that freed me.

One night, he told me he was sick of me looking like an old woman and wanted to see my legs. He also told me he hated my hats. All of them. (Well, ok, not all of them, but 99% of them.) So, I asked him to show me which suits he liked. There were five. I had all five skirts cut short to hit above my knee. I shaved my legs, oiled them up, and stopped wearing stockings and pantyhose. I only wore tights in the winter when it was cold. My skirts were short, and my jackets were cropped. Do you see the pattern? I wore clothing that allowed my husband to see my legs because he said I had gorgeous legs. That's right: I ditched the hats, the long shiny suits, and the old lady shoes. My pastor husband was ecstatic. And something happened when Tony Simon set me free: the other pastor friends of my husband decided Mrs. Laura L. Simon needed to have a chat with their wives.

Houston, we have a problem. If the PW doesn't know there's a problem with her long shiny suits, and her own pastor-man hasn't told her there's a problem with her long shiny suits, then how is Laura Simon going to convince her that there's a problem with her long shiny suits? See, here's the thing – some PW's and women in leadership *like* those long shiny suits. They think they look "sharp." Nope. They don't. They look a mess—a hot mess. They look dated and old.

My children were right. Those suits made *me* look like a walking couch. I looked like I was wearing upholstery. And it doesn't matter the size. If you're a small PW, then you just look like a s small couch, a settee, if you will. Ample PWs like me, well, either way, you're walking upholstery. My pictures speak for themselves. Now don't go and get all offended on me. Just stop. Simply ask your husband what *he* likes, and what he likes to see on *you*. Remember, your first ministry is your man. Your husband. Not your friends, and not the other pastor's wives. We don't count. So, just ask *him* what he likes. You may find out that he wants to see your legs too. And I bet if you ask him, and he's totally honest with you, he'll tell you he wants to see you in more form fitting outfits that don't resemble a couch.

Back to my cousin. After I changed from wearing "regalia", my attitude changed as well. I found that I was no longer snappy with the church folks; I became a much nicer person. Now all of this wasn't because of my style of dress, but the majority of it was. You see, I wasn't catering to the expectations of the members or the crowd anymore.

I was beginning to change on the inside and do things that were pleasing to God and to my husband. You'll discover when you do that, life becomes less taxing and burdensome. You begin to get excited about ministry again. You don't have to try on 18 different outfits trying to find the right one to wear to church. You don't have to worry about keeping up with the Joneses. You just want to help build the kingdom and be a good disciple for Christ.

Romans 12:1-2 in The Message Bible says exactly what I'm trying to say to you:

> "So, here's what I want you to do, God helping you: Take your everyday, ordinary life—your sleeping, eating, going-to-work, and

walking-around life—and place it before God as an offering. Embracing what God does for you is the best thing you can do for him. Don't become so well-adjusted to your culture that you fit into it without even thinking. Instead, fix your attention on God. You'll be changed from the inside out. Readily recognize what he wants from you, and quickly respond to it. Unlike the culture around you, always dragging you down to its level of immaturity, God brings the best out of you, develops well-formed maturity in you."

This is good. When we give our everyday life to God, He turns it around for us. If we're wearing things to please the crowd, the members, our family, or our friends, then we've got the wrong agenda. Our focus must be only on pleasing God. Maturity comes when we're able to wear what we want and what makes us comfortable and tell others or show others that it's okay to be ourselves.

When I became comfortable enough to wear what I wanted to wear, I was approached by other pastor's wives and women in leadership regarding my change. They wanted to know how I was able to make that transition.

At first, I wasn't kind because folks came at me in different ways. During a church service one Sunday, I stepped outside and had a few words with a member. She had said one of my children was stupid, or something to that effect. And for whatever reason, that morning I just wasn't feeling it, and her unthoughtful criticism struck a nerve – a big one, and I asked her,

"What would make you say that? I would like to know what would make those words come out of your mouth to me? I want to know, because I would never say anything like that to one of your kids."

She stared back at me in utter bewilderment. She couldn't believe I had just said that to her. I continued, "Why are you looking like that? Surprised? Didn't think I would answer you or say something back to you?"

Then I took a deep breath and went on, "Listen, just like *you* can say things to *me*, I can say things to *you*. So, you let me know when you're ready to talk about why you said that awful statement to me and why you thought it was ok to do so." She stuttered and said some words that I didn't quite understand, and then apologized. I immediately told my husband after church. He was like "Wow, sometimes you just have to tell 'em."

After a while, I learned to answer with more self-control. I'm not proud to say that my reputation for cutting throats if you said something crazy to me was spreading throughout the city, and I didn't like that even if it was true. I mean, I didn't see myself like that, and I didn't want other people to view me as such either. So, I made a conscious effort to change my attitude, and change my way of speaking to people; not just the members of the congregation, but to everyone in general. I asked God to help me temper my conversations and sprinkle all talks with love. He did just that.

When members would say things that were inappropriate, I would in turn say, "Wow, that's kinda harsh don't you think?" Basically, I would turn the tables on them, and make them think about what they said. "Was that nice?" You know, questions like that that made the other person feel bad. Okay, I didn't mean it that way; that sounds bad, so let me reword it. I would ask questions that would make them think about how their conversation made me feel. What did it accomplish for them? And then I would ask, "And what made you say that? Why do you feel that way if I may ask?" I even learned to use a much gentler (sigh) tone. This turns everything back to that person, and it allows him or her the opportunity to come up with either the truth or a big, fat lie we could both laugh out loud about. That usually breaks the tension between us, and we can then have the hard conversation on a new footing. My new mantra is this: everything can be said but it isn't always expeditious to do so. Think before you speak. Take a moment.

~

We are all parts of the body of Christ, but we do not have the same job. We all can't be the neck; somebody has to be the elbow. There's a way to say what has to be said. Earlier in the ministry I would be just as real and raw as I am today, but I didn't have the maturity to temper how my words came out. Now I may say the same things, but I ask the Holy Spirit what to say and how to say it. That makes all the difference in the world.

My grandmother would always say to me, "You get more flies with honey than vinegar," and she was right. Clothe your words in humility. Your words spoken with kindness get you much further than when they are laced with bitterness and sarcasm.

What do you mean, Laura?

Look, when I changed the way I dressed, I got a lot of haters, and they said some of the ugliest things out loud. And at that time my response would be, "And what made you say that?" That retort would often take them aback, then I'd add, "You said that to say what? What exactly are you trying to communicate to me? Because I wouldn't say that to you about anything."

I like 1 Thessalonians 5:14-15 which says, "Be patient with each person, attentive to individual needs. And be careful that when you get on each other's nerves you don't snap at each other. Look for the best in each other, and always do your best to bring it out." Plenty of people didn't understand why I went away from the hats and the shiny suits, but after gently explaining my new thought process, sometimes there was an understanding, and other times there was not. My dear cousin said I wasn't dressing or doing my best for the Lord because I was choosing not to wear the traditional garb. I remember the conversation just like it was yesterday.

"Laura, I give God my best," she said with a smile.

And I came back with, "And you're saying I don't? Because I choose not to wear the regalia, I'm not pleasing God or I'm not as holy or saved as you?" Then I got hot. "Girl, so let me get this straight: I'm not giving God my best?"

She backpedaled, "I mean, in the South and back in the day you wore your best to church."

Again, I responded, "So my wearing a skirt without stockings is not giving God my best?" Then I just went in, meaning, I let her have it. "This is why people don't want to come to church. This is why people say we are hypocritical and judgmental. Not everybody can afford to dress up in the southern-look-good-for-Jesus-regalia like you. Not everybody wants to dress like you. Like *that*," as I pointed to her long shiny suit. "And who are you to say that wearing slacks, or a skirt, or a simple dress is not giving God your best? This is why everyone needs to check their motives, their own agendas, and their own hearts when talking about what's best for God. Don't do that. Ask God what He judges as what your best is for Him and don't worry about what's best for me. If it's not hindering me from getting into the kingdom, leave it alone. Leave me alone about what I wear to church."

With that, our conversations about what we wear to church ended. She still wears her regalia to this day, and I don't. I think God is just fine with that.

Do you, but don't offend. Remember, this is your journey, and we each have our own path to take. Let's learn to get along and see each other the way God sees us—through the blood of Jesus. I know I took the long way around for this clothing topic, but it's close to my heart; really close. Like close, as in my immediate family still debates sleeves versus bare-arms-sleeveless. Let's not run people away with what to wear or what not to wear to church. Let's get people in the church first, then worry about how they dress later.

~

Questions to ask yourself and think about:

1. Why do you wear what you wear? Really think about it. I want you to be honest with yourself: Is it to show off? Is it to make a point? Do you offend people? Do you think more highly of yourself than you ought because of your style of clothing? Are you judgmental?

Do you think because you wear the traditional "garb" you're "better" than others? Journal your answers and thoughts. Then ask God to help you with your heart and show you the areas where you need help.

_____
_____
_____
_____
_____
_____
_____
_____
_____
_____
_____
_____
_____
_____
_____
_____
_____
_____
_____
_____.

What's one thing that has happened in your life about which you are judgmental? Do you even know? Ask yourself how has it shaped your thoughts and/or actions about certain beliefs.

_____
_____
_____

_____
_____
_____
_____
_____
_____
_____
_____
_____
_____
_____
_____
_____
_____
_____
_____
_____
_____
_____
_____
_____.

Read Romans 12:1-2 and 1 Thessalonians 5:14-15. Journal what it says to you after meditating and reflecting on it.

PRAYER

Lord, wow, I never really thought about being a judgmental person. God, search my heart and show me the areas in which I am judgmental. Help me to change my thought process and look to You for guidance. When I turn my nose up or say things in my heart about people based on what they wear, stop me, remind me of where I came and what I used to wear...then rein me in. In Jesus Name.

DID SHE SAY THAT OUT LOUD?

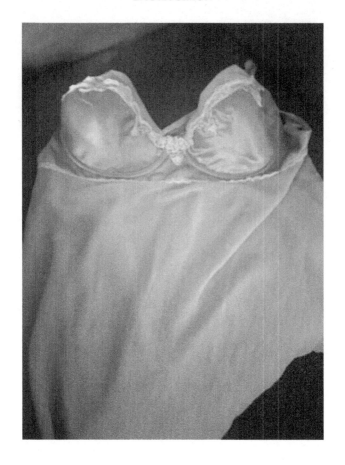

Chapter 3
So, You Just Stopped By

"Ohhhhhh. Mommy, that's preeeeety," sighed my four-year-old. She was in total awe and fascination as she followed me from room to room upstairs in our new house. I had "intimate issues" planned for her daddy and me that she didn't understand, but she knew there was something special about the outfit I was wearing.

I was a sheer vision of *lavenderness*—lavender and lovliness. Lavenderness. I had the body and boobs to make it pop. The A-line negligee was a flattering fit and draped nicely, leaving little to the imagination, right down to an ever-so-sexy piece of material that doubled as a thong. I thought I was hot stuff. And so did my daughter.

As I strolled in and out of each room, I was practicing my walk and rehearsing my lines. Kennedy would either walk behind me, or run around me, and walk backwards in front of me repeating the phrase, "Mommy, that's preeeety." Then she would touch the hem of the negligee and ask, "So where are you going?" I would stop and tell her, "Mommy's not going anywhere. I'm just trying this on to show Daddy how it looks on Mommy."

That seemed to satisfy her, although she remained quite transfixed with the color and fabric. Purple was her favorite color and the chiffon reminded her of the dresses worn by some of her Barbies. One huge difference, though, was the fact that Mommy's outfit was see through. Kennedy learned a new vocabulary word: sheer. And no matter how many times I said the word sheer, she insisted upon calling it "pretty purple see through."

We had only been in the house about six weeks. It was April 1999, and Tony told me we needed to start working on a sibling for Kennedy, otherwise our darling little girl would be an only child. We were both 34 and that dreaded 35 was quickly approaching, so he was saying he didn't want to be an old father. He had decided he wasn't having any kids after 35. Ha! He would live to eat that statement.

Anyway, with that thought in mind, I began preparing to get the second child. One of the steps of preparation was reading *Intimate Issues*, a relationship book written by authors Linda Dillow and Lorraine Pintus. Transparency moment here: the book is a Christian sex guide. Yes, I said it. And I said it out loud.

"Hi, my name is Laura and I'm a Book Addict." I'm not even a recovering Book Addict, but a full-fledged will-buy-any-book-at-any-time-in-any-form addict. Hard cover, paperback, kindle, it didn't matter. If I sensed an inkling of an interest, the book was mine.

I'm putting this out here right now because I need you to know I was in a season of buying Christian sex guidebooks. I bought one and told my pastor wife cousin to purchase one as well so we could read the book together and then try out the suggestions detailed in the book with the husbands. I figured we both needed to up our game and surprise our men.

She was on the ultra-conservative end of the sex spectrum, and I was somewhere closer to the not-so-conservative. I was trying not to collect any more t-shirts and end up on the wear-a-t-shirt to bed end of the spectrum. About seven months prior, my mom had thrown away all my not-sexy-at-all-night-time-bedroom-t-shirts. She also "voluntold" me not to wear t-shirts to bed anymore. So, "the lavenderness" was in anticipation of the end-of-the-book-assignment.

Let me put a pin right here so you have time to get a highlighter for this next bit of information. It's for free, as some of our husbands say when preaching. My mother said she knew she had taught me better. She didn't know why I needed all those books about sex when I just needed to step up my lingerie drawer. She could say this to me because that's what my father did. He bought her sexy lingerie for holidays and special days like their anniversary, her birthday, Christmas, and Mother's Day. He bought them in an array of colors—all see through. But here's the kicker—I had accompanied my dad to this swanky lingerie store in the mall for years. As I write this, it's all coming back to me! I understood why Kennedy was so infatuated with my lavenderness; I had been enthralled with all my mom's bedroom ensembles, too.

OK. Note to self: no boring outfits to bed. See through or nothing at all.

Alrighty then.

So, I was feeling pretty great about myself and decided to just walk around upstairs for a while until I was totally comfortable with my look, my walk, and my lavenderness. When I felt the time was right, I came out of our bedroom at the end of the hall and started walking to the stairs. Guess who met me halfway down the hallway? Yep, Kennedy. And one last time she grinned and said, "Mommy, that sure is preeeeety." And again, I answered, "Thank you Kennedy," and continued towards the stairs.

I was feeling good. I was feeling confident. I was feeling sexy. When I hit the top step, I didn't want to lose my nerve, so I walked down the stairs quickly, and as my right foot hit that 10th stair of 14, I saw her.

Too late.

I saw her—a church member. She was sitting at my brand-new dinette table, in my brand new eat-in kitchen, next to my brand new family room, in my brand new house.

"Uhhhhh," boobs all out, see through lavenderness, shiny smooth legs, church member seated at the dinette, and pastor husband sitting on the couch, "Hi Reba." I sat down on the 10th step.

"How ya doing?" What else could I do but start a conversation?

"Good, First Lady."

"So, you just stopped by?"

"Yeah. I was in the neighborhood, and I said, "Imma, just stop by."

"Oh. Ok."

"I know the housewarming isn't for a while, but since I was at Target, and I kinda knew where the house was, I just stopped by."

"Ah huh."

Reba obviously was unable to read the room. She just kept sitting right where she was and continued the conversation. "Yeah, I was looking for stuff for the wedding…"

I just sat on those steps, looking at her with my boobs out, legs all shiny, in my lavenderness.

"…but I figured it wasn't too late cause it's still early."

"Yeah. It's only 8:30 at night. But it *is* a Saturday night. We have church tomorrow…"

"Oh, I'm not gonna stay long. I was just in the area."

Forty-five (45) minutes later, I am still sitting on the 10th step, boobs out, shiny legs, see through lavenderness…

Reba's mouth rambles on. "And then my mom who's cooking for y'all, she made those turnovers and some greens…"

"Oh, that's great. I love your mom's turnovers and greens."

"And then my sister said…"

And I just sat there in all my lavenderness. But guess who finally reappeared at the top of the stairs? Yes, Kennedy. And while said church member was talking to her pastor, Kennedy started coming down the stairs. I turned around to face her and mouthed, "Why didn't you tell me Miss Reba was here?"

"Huh?" Kennedy wasn't understanding what I was saying to her.

Pointing my finger toward our "guest," again I mouthed the question, "Miss Reba."

In classic 4-year-old manner, Kennedy said aloud,

"I can't hear you."

Eye roll.

"Mommy, what did you say?"

I whispered, "Why didn't you tell me Miss Reba was here?"

"I don't know."

And so, I just turned around and sat there on the 10th step in all my glory.

Miss Reba stayed another 30 minutes. I sat on those stairs of an hour and 15 minutes! I didn't have the nerve to turn around and get up. The picture of my lavenderness, overflowing boobs, and shiny legs, would have been accompanied by my thonged booty. I couldn't do that, so I just sat there as lady church member continued to talk to pastor, and occasionally would turn around and include me. I guess she figured if the First Lady can sit there and talk as if she's fully dressed, then I can sit here and talk too.

Needless to say, there went the romantic night. When she finally got up to leave, I said from the step, "So glad you stopped by."

"Me, too," she cluelessly replied. "See you tomorrow at church."

With that, Tony walked her to the door, while I remained on the 10th step, boobs out, shiny legs, and all my lavenderness. But, oh, when the door shut, I got up, walked up the stairs, and stopped at Kennedy's room. I peeked my head in and said, "Kennedy, why didn't you tell me Miss Reba was downstairs? You see Mommy had on this outfit!"

The four-year-old simply answered, "I forgot. And you look soooo preeety, Mommy."

How could I be mad at that.

When Tony came back in, he hollered up to me, "She's gone!"

I retorted, "Doesn't matter! Do you know Kennedy knew she was here?"

Tony answered walking up the stairs, "Yeah, she knew. She talked to her."

"For real? I never would've come downstairs in this!"

"I was wondering what you were doing and where you were going."

My side-eye could have sliced him in two.

"How come you didn't get up and change?"

"And do what? I was embarrassed."

"Didn't look like it."

"Well, I was. But I didn't want Reba to know it. So, I sat there."

"Well, you played it off well."

"Thank you, Babe." My comments were dripping with sarcasm, but Tony wasn't reading the room either.

"What made her stop by unannounced?" He had to be kidding.

"I have no idea. I told you we should've moved to a gated community."

"I told you I didn't want to move to a gated community."

"Well, if we had, we wouldn't have had *this* situation happen."

"We can just not answer the door."

"Sounds good to me."

People coming to the house unannounced would be an issue for me until year eight of the ministry. That was the year I got pregnant with Jonathan, my youngest. I was 37 years old, headed to 38. And 38 is old to be pregnant. Okay, okay, I hear some of you saying no, no, it isn't. But when your friends are having grandchildren at 38 and you're having your last one, yeah, you're feeling old.

I digress…

It came to me that I needed to put my foot down and set some boundaries. PastorMan wasn't particularly thrilled, but I couldn't stand people just popping in or dropping by just because. I took his suggestion to heart and stopped answering the door. Now don't get me wrong, on some days those children of mine would answer the door anyway, but for the most part, the members got the message. I actually said to people, "I am old, and I am pregnant and I am tired. If you plan to stop by and see the pastor, please call or text first. That way you'll know we're home, and you'll know we'll answer the door. Should you come by without saying anything, you are subject to not be let in."

I found it was best to just tell people the truth. It saved hurt feelings, and it saved me from being so mad I wanted to cuss folks out.

Hospitality was and still is a strong suit of mine. However, as people began to abuse their agendas, I came up with one of my own: Don't. Answer. The. Door. End of story. Problem solved.

That was then, this is now.

The issues from 2004 are now handled in this manner, "Be patient with each person, attentive to individual needs. And be careful that when you get on each other's nerves you don't snap at each other. Look for the best in each other, and always do your best to bring it out." 1 Thessalonians 5:15 MSG

Although my version of that verse is worded just a

wee bit differently. Actually, I'd change it just a tiny bit. *And be careful when **they** get on your nerves.* Inevitably it will happen, and the thing to do is ask God for wisdom and patience on what to say and how to say it. He will help you see the best in those who are dancing around on that last nerve.

~

Reflection Time

1. What were your thoughts about the drop by situation?

2. How would you have handled it? What would you have done? What would you have said?

3. Do you have any boundaries set up with your spouse when it comes to your home? Your children? Your time?

4. Write out 1 Thessalonians 5:14-15 your way and in your voice. Share your new translation with a friend.

5. Journal your responses to the questions and download or brain dump (shout out to Cledra Gross, my Pastor's Wives' Life Coach) any particular feelings you have that you need or want to share. Get it all off your chest.

PRAYER

Lord, help. Help me to be more like You. Let me see the best in everyone, even when they get on my nerves or just stop by. Give me the strength to set boundaries and the courage to share with others my boundaries when it comes to taking care of myself, my husband,

and my children. In Jesus Name.

DID SHE SAY THAT OUT LOUD?

Chapter 4
It's Official: I'm A Pharisee

W ho picked this place?" I looked around suspiciously.

"We're having the awards banquet here?" My husband answered me excitedly, like he had just walked me into the swankiest hotel in the city. It was anything but.

"There wasn't another place to have the banquet?"

"Laura, it's just another place to eat."

"Well what kind of food are we having?" I shot back.

"Wings and other stuff kids like."

"Well, I'm not comfortable having my kids eat here. They're going to be asking questions. What are people going to think?" I whined.

"Laura, it's a restaurant. We're going to eat food and give out awards. Everyone will be fine. I promise."

"Well, I still don't like it. I don't want my boys or my girls looking at all these women serving them wings." I whispered now, looking around to see if the kids or any other parents heard me.

"Laura, it's just a restaurant," my pastor-husband whispered back.

"No, it's not, it's Hooters!" and sat back with arms folded. "Look at the boys. Look at the girls…" my voice trailed off. "I can't believe we are sitting here for a banquet." I seethed. Cue eye roll.

"I'll talk to the boys; you talk to the girls. It's just a restaurant, and it's just food. Get over it," and he was done discussing the subject.

Oh, my stars, I was in a panic. Here I sat, with about 60 people, half of whom were children under the age of 10, sprinkled with a few 12-year-olds. In my mind, this was just not the place to bring children or have a sports banquet for kids. So what it was a sports bar and restaurant. So what the food was pretty good. So what it was large enough to hold all levels of the basketball league and their parents. So what it was hosted at a very reasonable price. So what. It was *still* Hooters.

I tried my best to play it off and look comfortable like I was one of the other parents. Nobody else seemed to be bothered or upset about us being at Hooters except for me. Everyone was laughing and having a wonderful time. I was the only one looking around and checking to see if the boys and girls were staring at the servers. Some were and some weren't. Actually, the kids were more interested in the wings, the ranch dip, and trying to figure out who was going to get what award. The boys, if I'm honest, really weren't paying that much attention to the servers because for the most part they were covered up. I mean, the shorts were short, but not indecently short. The tops were kind of tight, but not super tight. Actually, the servers were wearing t-shirts. Maybe one or two were wearing Hooters tank tops. And the server girls wore those thick, flesh colored pantyhose that looked more like rest-home compression gear than sexy-come-hither stockings. In my head I had a checklist -- scantily clad: Hmmm. Old-Folks-Home-Looking-Stockings: Check. Better-shaped-bodies-than-mine: Yep. Any real good excuse not to have the banquet there: No. Here's a free definition of what was going on in my mind and heart: An excuse is a lie disguised as a reason.

As I sat there, the Holy Spirit quietly began to work on my heart. Alright, I'm going to be honest; might as well be. God started talking to *me*. Working on *me*. As He worked on *me*, my heart began to soften, and I started to loosen up and talk to the ladies who were assigned to serve our tables for this awards banquet. They were friendly, attentive, outgoing, and got along well with the kids. They made us feel quite comfortable, and after a while, the atmosphere (on my part anyway), lightened up. After all, I was the only one sitting there with my face all scrunched up, my arms folded, and stomach growling because of my stupid thought process and attitude.

The adults were having comfortable conversations with the servers telling them about our basketball league. The parents and players were telling the servers how and why my husband started coaching. And the servers and managers were genuinely interested.

Everyone was engaged in basketball and food conversations, and I began to feel convicted. Then the discussions got better: my sons decided to tell the people at Hooters what their dad did for a living besides coach. Yep, they told the servers their dad was a pastor. They were so proud. And so was I.

I felt proud, but I was also beginning to feel ashamed. Here I was, wife of the coach and pastor worrying about what people might be thinking or would possibly say. The pastor, his wife, and their kids had dinner at Hooters. They even had the audacity to have their kids' banquet there. Yeah. All this stuff spun around inside my head and inside my heart. I was the one having the issue. Nobody else said anything. Everybody was having a good time. The parents and employees were amazed at how "regular" Tony the Coach-Pastor was. How non-judgmental he was. Oh, and how nice his wife was.

"You guys are so regular."

"You don't act like a pastor."

"You don't act like a pastor's wife."

Ugh. I felt as if the word "hypocrite" was etched on my forehead, or at best, tattooed on both cheeks. These girls were just trying to make a living. An honest living. Some of them were college students. A few of them were single mothers trying to make it work, and all of them were extraordinary women supplementing their day job incomes. I say extraordinary because it takes a special person to hold down two jobs and be happy and nice about it.

And then there was me. Feel free to insert your long sigh right here. The hypocritical-spiritual PW who knew better. Insert your I-can't-believe-her with your raised eyebrows and hmmmm sound. May I just insert your "Wow" right here? There I was, hoarding the greatest award—Jesus, and I was too judgmental and afraid to share. Yes, afraid. Fear gripped my mind as I listened to my eight-year-old son talk about his father, how well he preached, and that they should come to our church, while I sat there in stunned silence. And a child shall lead them. Then my daughters chimed in with "Mom, we want to work here when we go to college."

"Okay," I said. Whatever face you imagine me having during this conversation is probably spot on.

"Mom, we can make some extra money!" they said excitedly. Like college was only a few seconds away.

"That's nice." I don't believe my forced smile was fooling anyone.

Nobody was being judgmental except for me. I had to be honest—I was hiding my light under the guise of concern for the children. What was really going on wasn't concern about the kids at all. I was just straight-up being judgmental. I had made an assumption about the Hooters' girls, and I was wrong. Instead of worrying about their outfits and what they were wearing and not wearing, I should've been showing them the love of Christ. My children were over there witnessing and being all spiritually mature, and I was having my own petty and juvenile, disapproving conversation with God.

Thankfully, God cut me off and started telling me to show them that being a Christian isn't all stiff and boring. He wanted me to show them Christians can and do have fun. "Show them, Laura, that you are not all judgmental or so holy that you can't have a nice meal with your family."

Hooters, like other restaurants, is a place where believers can have conversations. Meaningful conversations. Real conversations. Transformative conversations. This is where God can do some of His best work—in the uncomfortable places of our well-intentioned lives. But we can sometimes hinder Him with our attitudes. Sometimes as PW's or women in leadership, we have the tendency to act some type of way.

Alright, let me explain. Hooters wouldn't have been and wasn't my first choice for an Awards Banquet. But what was my rationale? What was my reasoning? Or better yet, let's just be honest, ok? I didn't want the banquet at Hooters because I thought it was a restaurant for single straight men and married men on the prowl. In other words, I had seen Hooters as nothing more than a Gentlemen's Club disguised as a respectable eating establishment.

And there's more.

My other shameful thought was that Hooters was a lesbian's dream come true. Okay, I said it because it's what I thought. And you can agree or disagree with me but go back and examine your heart and your thoughts. What's the real reason you don't want to have brunch, lunch, or dinner at Hooters?

Or maybe Hooters isn't your challenge. Alright smarty pants, whatever or wherever your uncomfortable place is, what's your reason? I'll wait. Oh, and one more thing I didn't say, but I'm saying now—I didn't want my husband looking at another woman whose body might just be in better shape than mine. Yes ma'am. Not so sure I wanted to see that. Not so sure I wanted him to see that. Okay. Your turn.

_____

_____

_____

_____

_____

_____

It doesn't have to be long. Just start with the truth. It's rough. I know. Go back and write it down.

It's hokie, but I often quote the saying, "Sometimes you are the only Bible some folks get to read." So, you can't very well be a fake Bible, can you? When God reminds you that you represent Him to the world, you should listen and be obedient when prompted by the Holy Spirit to watch how you come across to people. While God is working on your heart, work on working on others. Just like that? Yup. Just like that. I love that. "Be alert servants of the Master, cheerfully expectant...help needy Christians; be inventive in hospitality" 1 Thessalonians 5:11-13.

How can you be inventive in hospitality? First of all, be a servant. It's not about you. Step out of your box, your comfort zone, your comfortable place of piousness. Now this is hard. It's hard because it's something you don't want to easily admit. You really don't want to admit it at all. We have the tendency to be holy; so holy we are no earthly good. But Sisters, we can sometimes get beside ourselves with our righteous indignation. That was me. How dare we be at Hooters with the kids. God is not happy with this separatist arrogance. God is not happy with us. Take a chance on doing things God's way and step out on faith. Faith it 'til you make it.

God is everywhere and God is at Hooters. And while I was at Hooters what do you think God wanted me to do? Yes. He wanted me to talk to the people. And look what happened to me when I got a grip on myself: something wonderful. I was able to share the love of

Jesus with not only the Hooters Staff, but with the basketball parents. When those parents saw us eating, drinking, and laughing without any hesitation with the place, they wanted to know this God we served. They wanted to come to church and hear Tony share a message of hope, love, transparency, and authenticity. When people see the goodness of God in our lives, they want to learn more about this life we live for Jesus. Acting like we're "holier than thou" will offend or be a turn off for the potential believer.

We have since made Hooters a staple of our Eating Ministry. We've gone alone, Tony and I, and we've gone with the kids. When Kennedy was a freshman at UC Davis, we took our four kids and Kennedy's friends (10 in total) there for a late-night dinner. Her senior year, we again went to Hooters for a pre-graduation Last Supper. We have some of the best conversations there. And what have we learned? What have our children learned? We've all learned that places of discomfort for the believer can be life giving and life changing opportunities for the non-believer, or the backslider, or even the new believer.

If your children are small, answer their questions if they have any. Or talk about what's appropriate to wear and not to wear, and why the servers are wearing what they are wearing. What's a uniform? Have the life changing conversations. The world is showing your children what it wants them to learn, why not you show them what you want them to learn and get ahead of the world?

God wants no man to be lost. How do we become the hands and feet for our Father? By being better servants. Let's become better servants and "love from the center of who you are; don't fake it...Get along with each other; don't be stuck up. Make friends with nobodies, don't be the great somebody." Romans 12:9-10; 15-16. You can't talk to people about the love of Christ or share your Jesus journey with them if you're being judgmental, hypocritical, or supercilious. You can't demonstrate the love of Jesus sitting there with your arms folded or rolling your eyes. The judgmental "I'm-just-not-going-to-say-anything-at-all silence" will never win anyone to the Lord. It's just not possible. Ask yourself if you're acting like Jesus or more like a Pharisee.

~

Question of Reflection

Are you a Christian snob? Are you stuck up? Are you better than others? Do you believe your sin isn't like somebody else's sin—your sin is not as bad? Why are you avoiding certain places? Why are you afraid of the hard conversations? Afraid of what people might think? Afraid of what *you* think? Meditate on Romans 12:9-16. What is this passage saying to your heart?

_____

_____

_____

_____

_____

_____

_____

_____

_____

_____

_____
_____
_____
_____
_____
_____
_____
_____
_____
_____
_____
_____Ask, "Lord, how can I be
more like You? What areas of my heart need
transformation or change?"

_____
_____
_____
_____
_____
_____
_____
_____
_____
_____
_____
_____

PRAYER

*Lord, I don't want to be like the Pharisees –
hypocritical and judgmental. Help me to be more like
Christ and see the best in folks. When the hard*

situations, or hard conversations come up in my life, help me see them as opportunities to share with others about Your love. Let my light shine so men will ask about You. And when I get a little beside myself, and the Holy Spirit nudges my Phariseetical Heart, help me to hear from You and do the right thing...which is to love on Your children. In Jesus Name.

Chapter 5
What Happens in Vegas Stays in Vegas

A little groggy after a late night, I opened my eyes to a slight knock on the window, and footfalls hurriedly walking away. I sat up as I heard an engine rev and a quick "Bye." I fluffed my pillows, looked over at a sleeping Kennedy, and reached for Tony in the big king-sized bed. My thoughts tried to force my brain to awaken and make sense of the past few moments. *That's funny. That sounds like the Lockhart's car driving away.*

"Tony," I whispered, "Wake up. I think I heard the Lockhart's. I think they left."

"What?" Can't be. What did you hear?"

"I heard a faint knock on the window, a soft "bye," and then an engine." As I pulled back the curtain, I noticed I was right. "Look, the Lockhart's car is gone."

Tony looked out the window. "I told him not to hang out with Bradley. He must've lost all his money."

Tony dialed Bradley. "What happened? It looks like Lockhart left. What happened, Bradley?"

"Lockhart lost all his money and got mad. Said he wasn't staying and was going home. Least he waited 'til morning. I thought he was leaving last night."

"Well, he probably stayed over only because he already paid for the night."

"Yep. That's it."

And that's when we made the decision to test out anybody else who thought they wanted to go on a vacation with us; especially if it was to Las Vegas.

We aren't the typical Las Vegas people. Vegas' other name is Sin City, but we don't go for the sin, we go for the food. I guess too much food could be considered the sin of gluttony, but Tony and I are Vegas Foodies. We sample the various hotel restaurants, diners, drive-ins, and dives, as well as the little hole-in-the-walls. If it's a Vegas Buffet, Tony and I are there. So now when church folks want us to join them on any vacation, they have to answer a few questions before we give them a 'yes' answer:

1. Where are we trying to go?
2. How long is the trip?
3. Who all is going?

We don't even ask how much until those three questions have been answered satisfactorily.

Now it's known—if you go anywhere with the Simons, you are sworn to this rule: Whatever happens in Said City stays in Said City. We have been privileged to go to Las Vegas, Indianapolis, Arkansas,

Louisiana, Arizona, New Jersey, Texas, San Francisco, San Diego, and Mexico with quite a few of our church members. A beautiful time has been had by all.

But that wasn't always the case. The first few years of the ministry – 1996 – 1998—we were still new to the game and our thought process hadn't yet been tainted. The first church Tony pastored was filled with family and friends. Friends from elementary school, junior high, high school, and college for both of us filled our pews, as well as childhood church friends, as we came from two different Baptist churches in our hometown. So, in our minds, these were our friends, so why couldn't we go on a vacation with them? Yeah. No. Pastoring friends and family is one of the hardest things to do.

You don't believe me, or you already know?

In the Bible, Matthew and Mark both share their accounts of how Jesus couldn't do many miracles in His hometown because of the people's unbelief and familiarity; the familiarity wording is my own. First, here are the Bible verses related to the point above, and here's Laura's perspective:

> "Jesus told them, "A prophet has little honor in his hometown, among his relatives, on the streets he played in as a child." Jesus wasn't able to do much of anything there…he couldn't get over their stubbornness. He left and made a circuit of the other villages, teaching." Mk 6:4-6

> Matthew writes, "When Jesus finished telling these stories, he left there, returned to his hometown, and gave a lecture in the meetinghouse. He stole the show, impressing everyone. "We had no idea he was this good!"

they said. "How did he get so wise, get such ability?" But in the next breath they were cutting him down: "We've known him since he was a kid; he's the carpenter's son. We know his mother, Mary. We know his brothers James and Joseph, Simon and Judas. All his sisters live here. Who does he think he is?" They got all bent out of shape. But Jesus said, "A prophet is taken for granted in his hometown and his family." He didn't do many miracles there because of their hostile indifference." Matthew 13:53-58

The trip to Vegas solidified Matthew's and Mark's words. Friends and family are the hardest to pastor because they are stubborn and don't listen. Period. They love you and they want to follow you—they really think they do. But they don't follow you. Do you understand what I am saying? They really do think they want to follow your leadership, but they don't follow your leadership, which means they don't want to. They don't feel like it. And they don't means just that—they don't. They don't listen to what you say, and they don't follow your direction or vision even if it is right.

Now, I want you to keep what I have said in the back of your mind while you read the rest of this chapter. Let me set it up for you.

The Las Vegas caravan consisted of the pastor's family of three, the assistant pastor's family of four, the deacon's family of six, the minister of music and his newlywed wife, and a trustee and his very pregnant wife. Seventeen (17) people from the church headed to Vegas all ablaze in a Suburban, a midsized sedan, a compact, a small car, and a sports car. Everyone was so excited.

Pastor-Man set some guidelines. He told the group that his family came to Vegas to eat, sightsee, and shop. We didn't gamble. And if we did play the slot machines, we played the penny or nickel machine, and our budget was $20. When the $20 was gone, we were done. Twenty dollars is just enough money to make pennies and nickels look like a lot and losing that amount didn't make you feel like you broke the bank. Sometimes Tony and I only spent $10.

On one of our trips to Biloxi, Mississippi, we went to Harrah's Boat Casino on the river. Because it was a new casino, we were part of the grand opening and one of the perks was learning how to play all the games offered. I wanted to learn how to spin the Roulette Wheel and play Poker and Blackjack. I also wanted to try my hand again at Craps. We weren't good at any of them except Blackjack. Although I could keep a straight face, Tony and I both hated losing money, and the only thing I continued to play *alone* was Blackjack, because Tony was Schlep Rock from the Flintstones and was a loser at everything.

Another reason I continued to play Blackjack was because I was playing with house money. I won $150. Whoo! Talk about fun! That paid for our entire trip from Louisiana. We put gas back in the tank, ate dinner and breakfast, then drove back home with grocery money for the next week.

So, Tony tells Deacon Lockhart, "Let's go to dinner," but, no, the deacon wanted to hang with his brother-in-love, who was the assistant pastor and happened to have a really good job so he could spend a little bit. Well, Deacon Lockhart decided he definitely wanted to hang with him and try to win some money. Bwahahahaha! Not so!

One must understand the general rule in Las Vegas: money begets money. Money attracts more money, and against Tony's guidelines, restrictions, rules, and regulations, and against Tony's better judgment, Lockhart went on ahead and left his family in the room while he went with his brother-in-law downstairs to the casino. There Bradley proceeded to win big money while Lockhart proceeded to lose all his. That was the beginning of the end. Lockhart lost *all* their money for the trip, hence the hasty departure the following morning before sunrise. We just hoped he had enough cash for gas to get home, because his sister told us he literally lost all the money and was super mad. He honestly thought he was going to win like Bradley who was playing with more money and remember "mo' money begets mo' money."

It was a lesson learned for everyone. Friends and family believe they know you, and they feel as if they know you better than the regular church members do. But the other issue is people who went to school with you, or were your friends back when, or played with you in Sunday School at age five don't necessarily think you can pastor them.

And that thought leads me back to the beginning of this discussion. Member-friends and member-family think they don't need to listen to you. They think *So what you're the pastor. I know just as much as you do. As a matter of fact, I think I know more than you.*

And that's the problem. Tony told his friend, his deacon, his member, his family not to spend all his money. He told him to just wait until the next day. We also told him Vegas is a great place for families because food is inexpensive, and there's plenty of kid friendly entertainment. And, of course, there's fabulous adult fun too, so just wait.

By Lockhart leaving the next day, he and his family missed out on all the adventures. Their five-day trip condensed down to one. And it wasn't even one, because they didn't even experience 24 hours of Vegas. One of the best lessons missed was the trip to The Stratosphere. The remaining four families had the opportunity of a lifetime. That hotel was brand new at the time and had two thrill rides, two pools, and an arcade. The tourist selling point: all the fun stuff was on the rooftop of the hotel. It had the highest observation point in Las Vegas at a ridiculously scary height of 921 feet above the Strip.

Back to the lesson.

The reason I want to point out the facts about the Stratosphere is to show you how much influence our husbands have. We rode those thrill rides. What? Yes. Tony and I were also the avid rollercoaster–scary-ride-riding type. We convinced the men and one of the women to ride with us. Bradley's wife was a no-rollercoaster-riding woman. My soror (sorority sister) was also a no-rollercoaster-riding woman, but I convinced her to ride it once before she said no to the Big Shot.

Jennifer, our pregnant member said, "You both can't ride at the same time! If something happens to y'all, Kennedy will be an orphan," she pleaded.

"God will take care of us," we answered. See, that's youth and stupidity, and not an ounce of wisdom.

So not only did we ride the High Roller twice, but then we got on the Big Shot, and bought the pictures as a reminder to never do that again. Afterwards we went to the arcade for three-year-old Kennedy so she could ride the baby rollercoaster. That ride just happened to be inside, and the rest of us walked around and ate all the carnival-like treats.

This is what the Lockharts missed. If they—as friends, family, and members—can be influenced and listen to us about food, places, and rides, why won't they listen to us when it comes to tithes, offerings, and life applications? Because of their unbelief? No, I truly believe it's because they think they know us too intimately.

I agree with Jesus' take on his peeps in Nazareth. They had a bad case of the "unbeliefs." Surely our Jesus can't be who He says He is. He's Joseph and Mary's boy. To me, that's the same with our peeps. They watch us live life in the fishbowl. They see the things we go through. They walk with us through some of the valleys, yet, they still don't believe us when we tell them a truth or give them advice. Hence early departures or missed opportunities of a lifetime happen. Sometimes we aren't meant to be the ones who shepherd friends or family. But if we are, it's not an easy task, and it takes Godly balance and wisdom on everyone's part to make it work.

Deacon Lockhart later admitted he shouldn't have gone down to the casino with Bradley. He also said he shouldn't have left. During that season, life was good and all of us had a little bit of money. Had the Lockharts stayed, the other couples had planned to share and make sure everyone had a good time. But we were all robbed of the blessing. All because someone wouldn't listen.

Carefully choose your inner circle. Make certain the church-member-family-peeps are the ones who won't go back and tell. We're all human, but we need to make sure the humans we hang out with are humble. Their mindset should be one of compassion, understanding, and no judgment. The pastor and family are just like everyone else. They slip, they fall, and they have moments. And when they're caught up in those moments, that circle of friends shouldn't throw you under the bus to the other church members.

When we got back for church that Sunday after the Vegas trip, none of us mentioned that Deacon Lockhart returned home early. We all agreed that we had a good time and if the Lockharts wanted to tell their story, that would be their decision. Now did we laugh about it amongst our five families? Absolutely. But what happens in Vegas stays in Vegas.

~

Questions, Reflections, Things to Ponder

1. Do you have friends and family members in your congregation?

2. Who are they? How are they related?

3. Are there issues or problems when it comes to pastoring or mentoring them?

4. Why do you think it's so hard to shepherd those you know well or are close to?

5. Have you vacationed with any of your members? How did it go?

6. What would some of your vacationing rules be?

7. When thinking about your influence on others: Do you take it lightly? Do you take it for granted? Do you see a difference between church and home?

PRAYER

Lord, help me to choose the right friends to go on vacation with. In Jesus Name.

Chapter 6
Converted: But You Can Still Catch These Hands

The church members began to murmur.

"What's wrong with her?"

"She doesn't look happy."

"Did you hear what she told Sheila?"

"Girrrrl, she went off on Bro. Nelson. Sent him a note and told him to stop plucking that guitar!"

"Did you see her face?"

"Why does she always look mad?"

One night after church, one of the church ladies crossed the line, as in, she stepped *way* over the line. And I snapped. I asked her if I could speak with her in the back—the finance/storage/back-office office. I closed the door and locked it, and then began to scream and holler and hiss, "What the hell?" Then I proceeded to lay hands on her. Not a good night.

Both pastor-husband and church-lady-husband came banging on the door yelling, "Laura, open this door. OPEN THIS DOOR! Unlock this door!"

More bangs. More words. Meanwhile, I was having

an out-of-body experience and had zero intention of opening the door until I had said all that I wanted to say. And to add icing to the cake, the heated exchange was heard by just about every member that was still at the church, inside the church, or outside the church. No Bueno. Translation: Not good.

Well, it took a minute, but eventually I opened the door. I was in trouble. Serious trouble. That look the pastor gave me when I finally let him in was deadly, but church-lady-husband gave me the sista-I-understand look. He understood all right. He knew how his wife could be. But she was his wife and he basically lived by the motto "Happy wife, happy life." He was fine because he wasn't the one in trouble. Still, of course, she was not fine. (Insert eye roll.) They left the fellowship. (Cue dramatic music.)

I didn't care. So what. Farewell. Good riddance. Bye. I was sick of her anyway. Leave. See you later. Don't let the door hit ya, where the good Lord split ya. Don't ya come back, ya hear!

I see your open mouths and raised eyebrows through this page. You're thinking, "What? You said that?"

Don't judge me.

But my husband, the pastor did care.

As I was cooling off, I still held my ground for a while. I reasoned, "I helped the church and the Lord do some serious pruning. Um, hello, isn't that in my job description? No? Look, I'd had enough of church lady and her wayward sheep antics."

But that's just it—she was a sheep who was acting like a goat and maybe, just maybe, straightening her out was *not* in my job description as the helpmeet to the pastor.

I finally had to admit I was truly not running in my lane. And that, dear sister, was the night I took off all the masks I'd been wearing. All of them. All at once. All on the same day and all at the church.

After that I started wearing a new mask: Indifference. The indifference mask is also known as I-don't-give-a-good-*bleep-bleep* mask. And I really didn't. Those people didn't like me, and I didn't like them, and I didn't care. Those years of ministry were years I called the Dark Ages. And rightfully so. I was in a very dark place and didn't plan on coming out of it any time soon. Wore it proudly. Don't ask me anything and I won't tell you anything. That night, I replaced the old mask I had been wearing, put on the new mask of indifference, and erected a big, fat, tall wall that totally surrounded my heart. I wasn't going to hide and pretend anymore. Will the real Laura Simon please stand up? I did.

This was a turning point for me. A pivotal moment in my ministry. I felt liberated. Free. But that liberation and freedom came with a price. A hefty one. Did I tell you disobedience sucks? Yeah. Well, let me tell you something else—partial obedience is still disobedience. And disobedience kicks rocks. Big sigh. God told me I could talk to the Church Lady. What He didn't sign off on was how I should say what I needed to say, where to say it, and when to say it. He did give me permission to talk to her because she had been out of control for a very, very long time. But, oh, oh, oh, God had words for me when I got ready to listen to Him about the incident.

God: I did not tell you to do that.

Me: Yes, You did, God. You said I could talk to her!

God: Did I tell you to touch her, or yell at her like that?

Me: You said I could talk to her.

God: Answer the question.

Me: But, God, You said I could talk to her.

God: You still haven't answered My question.

As I sat in my room, on my bed, looking at Tony in his chair, I wrestled with God's questioning. I had no answer. Then the Pastor-Husband said, "Well, they've quit the church. They're leaving. Church-Lady Husband says he understands, but Church-Lady is very upset." So, my Pastor-Husband-Man continued, "You shouldn't have done that. I don't care what you wanted to do, or how you felt you were protecting me—it just wasn't right. And I can take care of myself, Laura. I'm a big boy. Now I have to clean *your* mess! You need to apologize to her."

Me: Absolutely not. I. Will. Not. Ain't gonna happen. God told me I could do it. He said I could say it, so I said it.

Tony: God did not tell you that. And now I have to clean it up, and they've left.

Me: Good. Bye. She shouldn't have disrespected you like that. Talking all loud and calling you stupid in front of the members. I don't care if she used to be your secretary or not. She shouldn't have said that, so I got her. Period. What goes around comes around. She's always running her mouth like she's so close to you and knows everything. She won't be saying nothin' else now, will she?

God: Did I tell you to do it like that?

Tony: But did God tell you to do it like that? I don't think He did!

Me: Oh well. Glad she's gone. Gonna miss her husband, though.

And that's the time I should've put on the mask that pretended I cared. There lies the difference between being authentic and just being disobedient. I was totally out of line. Even if she was wrong, I was wrong-er. And I owned it.

Eventually.

I called the Church-Lady to apologize. But I wasn't right. I didn't do it right or say it right. *Baaay*-bee, when I say Pastor-Man was still livid with me when I got off that phone that night, Pastor-Man was still livid with me when I got off that phone that night. I hadn't started to care. I was still wearing the I-Don't-Give-a-Bleep-Bleep mask, and this was my apology, "Church-Lady, I apologize for what I did, and how I said it. But I meant it. Every word. Do you accept my apology?"

What?

Church Lady: No. No, I do not.

Me: Ok. Bye. *Click.*

God: What was that?

Tony: What was that?

Me: An apology.

God: It was wrong.

Tony: That was wrong.

Me: I apologized.

God: Girrrrrrrrrrrl ...

Me: Alright. Alright. Give me another shot.

Tony: Laura that was not an apology.

Me: Whatever.

Now listen Sisters, I knew better. Let's talk present

tense. Even if the other person is wrong, we know what we should do. We know what is right, and we also know what is pleasing to God. And I knew. I had to get before God and do six weeks of praying, fasting, and crying out to Him. I was like the prophet Habakkuk in chapter 1, verses 2-5 of his book as he complained to God. "How long, Lord, must I call for help, but you do not listen? Or cry out to you, 'Violence!' but you do not save? Why do you make me look at injustice? Why do you tolerate wrongdoing? Destruction and violence are before me; there is strife, and conflict abounds. Therefore, the law is paralyzed and just never prevails. The wicked hem in the righteous, so that justice is perverted."

The Lord's answer to Habakkuk hit me between the eyes. "Look at the nations and watch – and be utterly amazed, for I am going to do something in your days that you would not believe, even if you were told."

God spoke to my heart through those verses and told me Church-Lady and her husband were His sheep and He could handle them just fine with my help. God also reminded me of some other scriptures that kept me in check. Romans 12:18-21 NIV says, "If it is possible, as far as it depends on you, live at peace with everyone. Do not take revenge, my dear friends, but leave room for God's wrath, for it is written: 'it is mine to avenge: I will repay' says the Lord. On the contrary, 'If your enemy is hungry, feed him; if he is thirsty, give him something to drink. In doing this, you will heap burning coals on his head. Do not be overcome with evil, but overcome evil with good.'"

Dang it. There went my excuse for my part in the adventure. Dang it. Dang it. Dang it.

Here's something else I want you to contemplate, mull over, think about, and seriously meditate on because the next truth is going to be in quite a few other chapters of this book. It's the definition I learned back in 1999 for the word "excuse."

An excuse is a lie disguised as a reason. I like that!

My part in this situation was not like Christ, nor was it right. I was out of line and not in my lane at all. I did not turn the other cheek or see the best in the Church-Lady. And I most certainly did not lean on God or trust in Him concerning how I should handle the situation. I totally did my own thing. I leaned on my own understanding, and I didn't even try to acknowledge the direction He was leading me.

So, yes, I know a little something-something about wearing masks and trying to hide the real me. And that's what we do. When I say "we," I'm talking about we pastor's wives, minister's wives, and women in leadership. We pretend and wear masks, and that's why we can't heal. We would rather wear the mask and pretend everything is fine, knowing full well we're not fine. We're acting like we can handle things well, but we can't, and we don't. We cannot handle this fishbowl-life-craziness on our own! We've got to start reaching out for help.

You've got to start reaching out for help.

You cannot do this on your own.

It's okay not to be okay.

And yes, I said that out loud.

~

Pondering Thoughts & Questions

Answer the following questions. Be sure to journal honestly. Ask God to help you take a good look at yourself.

1. What or who has made you snap?
    a. What triggered it?
    b. How did you handle it?
    c. What could you have done differently?
2. Are you okay or are you not okay about the above incident? Does it still bother you?
3. Right now, what do you need to give to God?
4. What human do you feel comfortable enough to share your feelings with?

~

PRAYER

Lord, You know what's bothering me, and You know the people who get on my nerves and make me snap. Help me to bring everything and everyone to You. Please encourage me to meditate on and hide in my heart 1 Thessalonians 5:14-15. Help me to be patient, kind, and give grace to those who trigger my attitude. God, I so want to be more like Jesus. Lead me in the way You want me to go and teach me to be see the best in everyone. And when I get in my own way, quickly arrest my attention, so I can say and do the right thing. I want to please You. In Jesus Name.

DID SHE SAY THAT OUT LOUD?

Chapter 7
Don't Help Me: I Hate the Village

D o you know what I hate most about the church peeps? When they try to help me with my kids or my husband. Now don't get me wrong. I love me some good help. When I was a younger pastor's wife, taking the kids for a few hours on Sunday was great. But now I know better. I should've never, never, ever handed them over to the church folks.

My sentiment, "Don't Help Me: I Hate The Village" is really up close and personal. I look back now and think, "Kennedy never should have spent the night with Sissy; Sagel never should've spent the night with Kevin; Sydni never should've stayed with Angie; and Jonathan should've had the opportunity to spend the night somewhere. Had I known what I know now, never ever would I have let any of my four children stay with other folks, church or otherwise.

When it comes to the pastor's kids, affectionately known as PK's, staying with, or hanging out with the church folks sometimes should just be an automatic no. As young parents, Tony and I didn't think of it that way. Not wanting to be judgmental or anything, we figured the kids should be around a myriad of people so they could learn how to get along with anyone and everyone.

Wrong.

The number one lesson learned: trust no one. Trust no one with your kids. Don't trust your family. Don't trust your friends. And don't trust the church folks. I don't care how holy they seem, how holy they look, or how holy they sound. follow them home. We have four children who have quite a few traits that we hate, mind you, and quite a few habits that we also hate our children have picked up from people other than us.

Yes, we hate that the village helped us with our kids, and yes, I said that out loud. Out loud. Whoo-wee! If I had money for all the times I sent my children to the Village's House, baby, I'd be a gazillionaire. What was I thinking? What were we thinking? Tony and I say, "If we could just do it all over again." When my mom told me the time would fly by while raising my children, I thought she was crazy. But she wasn't. The time flew by, and I have several regrets, but the time is gone, and I can't—we can't get it back.

What about you? Did the Village hurt you too? Some people who I thought had it together, did not. All sorts of stuff was going on at their houses. And, yes, I meant to say it just how I said it. I should've kept my babies away from their houses! Listen, if you have babies, toddlers, young children, or even older children at home right now (insert pause for dramatic emphasis), don't you let those kids spend the night at anybody's house. Period.

Period.

Not an option.

Don't do it.

You. Will. Live. To. Regret. It. Later.

Trust me.

At the first church my husband pastored, we had a Spanish ministry with a Latino pastor who had six children. Although the children ranged in ages from nine months to 12 years, that family was always together. He even drove an Econoline van—y'all remember those? It was a ginormous van that could seat 15 quite comfortably. Anyway, Pastor Jaime would never let his children spend the night with anybody, not even the Simons. Nope, wasn't going to happen. I don't care how long they stayed at our house swimming, playing, or having youth Bible study, at some point in time, no matter how late it was, they were packing it up and going the heck home. Home. And now 24 years later, I realize I never should've allowed my daughters nor my sons to spend the night at any of their friends' homes.

When it comes to rules and regulations and morals, listen here, everybody does not have the same moral compass. Know that. There's the holy roller-judgmental member, the idiot member, the perverted member, the know-it-all member, and the oh-so-sweet-just-want-to-help member. Beware especially of that last one. That's the one who usually has a houseful of dysfunctional other folks living with her and she "forgot" to tell you. *Insert wide eyes and perched lips.*

How do you handle those types of members? Very carefully is my first answer; however, truth be told, only God can tell you how that person has to be handled. I'm not giving you anything fancy or super holy, but wisdom says share, so I'm sharing. Sharing is Caring.

Next.

I shared a story at a conference about my husband and my oldest daughter. The story shocked a few of the attendees. But there's a rule Tony and I have in our marriage and in our family life: *transparency*, and it applies not only to us, but to our kids. Hear me well, okay? Being transparent isn't for the faint of heart. It also ain't for everybody. Now, I'm not saying that to put any one person or any people down, but what *I am* saying is not everybody wants to share. Not everybody wants to tell the truth about what goes on in their house. I need you to hear me! That is why, *pause*...this is why I was compelled, convicted, and *coerced* into writing books about the saga of pastor's wives. You *cannot* make this stuff up.

Laura, why did you tell us that? Because with transparency comes freedom, and with freedom comes haters. Haters don't like to see free people be free. Listen, if you are honest and transparent about your life, your kids, and you, you don't have to worry about remembering the lie or lies you told others to either make yourself look good or impress other folks. And this is for free: other folks know you are lying anyway. After you tell them lies and turn around and walk away, the people are already saying, "They lyin'." I promise, I promise people say that when you leave. Then the cruel part—the kicker to all this—is they remember what you said. They remember the lie you told them.

But you don't. And therein lies the problem with pastor's wives, minister's wives, women and men, heck, let's just say, people. We lie and forget the lie and then the lie comes back to bite us. Deliver me from the PW who gives her sanctimonious testimony or larger-than-life *(you fill in this space)* Bahama-Israel-Spain-Sweden-Hawaii-Dubai-Mexico vacation story or whatever grandiose claim she's claiming. Then she talks about how God sent someone to deliver them from whatever they needed to be delivered from that just happened to have been lied about during the sanctimonious testimony, larger-than-life *(you fill in the space)* Bahama-Israel-Spain-Sweden-Hawaii-Dubai-Mexico vacation, and grandiose claim that she claimed. Girl, Stop it! Just Cut. It. Out!

And that's why Tony and I are simply honest, transparent, and it-is-what-it-is type people. Saves us the grief. And I said all that because people hate your freedom. And because they hate your freedom, they tend to hate on you. And they will hate on your kids. Which brings me back to why I say, "I hate the village." People assume that because you're open, honest, and transparent, they can tell you about you, yourself, your spouse, and your kids. The reason I put "yourself" in that phrase is because I'm emphasizing how people judge you but forget about their drama at their house and in their family. In other words, they forget about the drama in them.

The other problem with the transparent thing is that people call themselves being transparent when they want to talk about you, but transparency all flies out the window when it's time to discuss their issues. Again, I hate the village. They mean well but inserting their feet into their mouths is more often the outcome of the situation.

The Village will take it upon themselves to give

advice, even though they don't live by their own advice, or use their own advice on their own kids. The other reason I hate the village is because they don't think or ask before they proceed with stupidness. Yes, stupidness. It's a word I made up.

Let's see, *(think of me with one eyebrow raised and my thumb and index finger on my chin)* Village Person decides he or she needs to tell the pastor's children or wife about an issue he or she feels he or she needs to address. That's the problem. He or she should consult God, as in, pray about it, and then approach the pastor, his wife, or their children, IF God says so. I can't speak for anybody else or their church, but I can speak for ours. Once said Village Person has made up his or her mind, just get ready for the stupidness.

Oh wait, before I get into that, I need to tell you: The Village can dish it out, but The Village can't take it. That's my disclaimer. The Village cannot handle push back. The Village will be quite upset if you ask, "What did you say?" or "Are you kidding me?" or "And you said that to say what?" or "What would make you write that?" or respond with any questioning of said stupidness. They. Cannot. Take. It.

One Village Person felt led to make a card, filled it up with scriptures, wrote an additional four pages of handwritten stuff about my daughter's lifestyle, and then hand-delivered it to my daughter. Village Person felt absolutely justified in doing so. I saw her hand the envelope to my daughter. I saw my daughter open the card with a puzzled then angry look as she read some of the contents. Then I watched my daughter march right on over to me with the Village Person's card. She said, "Mom, did you see Village Lady give me this?"

"Uh hm…I did."

"Mom, does she know she should be giving this to her own daughter?"

"Girl don't mind that. She calls herself helping you."

My daughter's eyes rolled, and I continued, "Plus, maybe she was practicing on you what to say to her own daughter."

I tried to keep my anger in check in front of my child, knowing full well I wanted to march over to Village Person and sock her in her neck. But I didn't. I also wanted to ask Village Person if she had already made, written, and given a similar card about the alternative lifestyle to her own daughter? But I didn't do that either. God told me to wait—that I would get a chance to chat with Village Person another time. Sunday was not the time.

Believe me, my anger was on simmer every time I saw Village Person until God let me know the time and place was right for this issue to be addressed. Eventually I was able to tell Village Person in a group setting that giving my daughter that card was offensive, judgmental, and wrong. She didn't believe me, of course, so I enlisted the aid of the group. To my delight (yes, I said it, no need to pretend I wasn't hoping the group would be on my side ☺), the rest of the group all agreed with me! God totally vindicated me on all three points. Her action was offensive, it was very judgmental, and it was most certainly wrong. But of course, I found out later she was offended by the group situation. Okay, I'll come clean. She was mainly offended by me. But I didn't care. I still don't. Like I said earlier, the Village can dish it out, but the Village can't take it.

Then there was the time when same said Village Person wanted to write my son a letter, but two good Village Persons put a stop to that. Thank God! Village Person is two for four when dealing with the kids, and one for two when dealing with me and PastorMan.

Don't think Village Person left us out. No ma'am. No sir. Village Person was an equal opportunity judger. Ha! She did eventually tell us she wrote her own daughter. But she didn't tell us all the particulars of what that letter was about. It amazes me how The Village wants to know and tell you all about your life but can't and won't tell you about theirs. Hmmm. I'm just going to leave that right there.

Do you hate The Village? Do I really hate The Village? No, really, I don't. But on some days, I wish they'd just try not to help me. Sometimes they do more harm than good, and the PastorMan, your PastorMan, or you or me is left holding the bag and having to make things right. Or not. I'm good for dropping the bag and handing it to my husband. He's so much better at resolving these kinds of issues.

What have I used to help me understand and do right by The Village? I remind myself of words written by Paul:

> "If you preach, just preach God's Message, nothing else; if you help, just help, don't take over; if you teach, stick to your teaching; if you give encouraging guidance, be careful that you don't get bossy; if you're put in charge, don't manipulate; if you're called to give aid to people in distress, keep your eyes open and be quick to respond; if you work with the disadvantaged,

don't let yourself get irritated with them or depressed by them. Keep a smile on your face."
Romans 12:6-8

The Village uses Romans 12 to justify the things they say to us. But Paul says it oh so clearly, just because you preach, or you teach, or you encourage, or you're in charge, or you give aid, or you work with the disadvantaged, don't think too highly of yourself and get crazy. Don't get so holy you get beside yourself and think you are better than others.

When you're doing right by people in The Village, but they don't do right by you, just remember not to get irritated or depressed. See The Village through the eyes of Christ and keep a smile on your face. God is with you, Sister Girls, and He will never leave you or forsake you, and He will help you deal with The Village. I promise.

~

Reflections, Questions, Things to Ponder

1. Do you have a Village?

2. What aggravates you most about The Village if anything?

    a. Maybe you don't have an issue. Acknowledge and write about that.

    b. What do you love about The Village?

3. Ask God to give you patience for The Village and how you should interact with them. Write down what He tells you.

4. A wisdom note: People will believe a lie faster than the truth, especially about those in ministry. Why do you think that happens? Write

out your answer and please email it to laurasimon@gmail.com. I actually plan to do research on the issue. Thank you for helping me.

PRAYER

Father God, I thank You for The Village. Help me to be more loving, more compassionate, and more like Jesus when I deal with The Village. Give me wisdom on when to speak and when to remain silent. Help me, oh God, as I want to please You. And when I serve The Village, help me not to be irritated, which is the lowest form of anger, or aggravated, depressed, or discouraged, or disappointed with them because of some of the things they say or some of the things they do. Lord, please help me to remember I must forgive them, just as You have forgiven me. In Jesus Name.

Chapter 8
Yes, That's Our New Car and I'm Driving It

"C an I drive it to church Sunday?" I gushed, standing outside of the Selman Chevrolet Dealership, admiring my spanking, brand-new Suburban.

"Nope. Not until after the anniversary," responded Tony. The celebration of the third Pastor and Wife Anniversary/Appreciation at the church was approaching.

"You know we can't drive up on the parking lot with this before the anniversary," said Pastor-Man with a slight grin. "Girl, you wanna cause a fight?"

"Well good grief, Tony, I'm six months pregnant with twins, you really think they'll have a problem?"

"Absolutely. We're not doing it. You're gonna have to wait until two weeks after the anniversary to drive this to church. Period." He was finished.

And that's when it started. Well, it started before then, but I figured since I was pregnant, it would make a difference.

It did not.

Let's go back a little so I can get you up to speed and have you join the conversation.

We had been at the church since 1994, and Tony became the senior pastor June 8, 1996. Our only child at the time was Kennedy, and we had already been through a few janky cars. The last one being an Astro Van. Do you remember that pointy nosed car that was the equivalent to the Space Shuttle? People even called it just that: The Space Shuttle.

Anyway, the pastor is always supposed to have a raggedy car, a run-down house, and unkept children.

"Nooooooo," I hear you saying.

"Yesssss."

The pastor's family is never supposed to have anything nicer than the parishioners. If they do, (insert right eyebrow raised, lip turned up at one corner) there's going to be a problem. Why? Because said parishioner is going to say things like:

"We pay the pastor too much money."

"He makes more money than I do!"

"Did you see what they are driving?"

"How can they afford that with what we're paying him?"

"Child, they don't need that."

And the list goes on forever. We just don't have enough time to go into every side remark, side-eyed, or downright petty discussion and statement. Just know that I know what I'm talking about. And even if you don't know, I know because it happened at our church.

Back to what I was saying. I had my first ectopic pregnancy in June of 1997. The ectopic pregnancy resulted in a rupture and removal of my right fallopian tube: more about that in chapter 16. Then, on May

1,1999 I got pregnant again. We found out at five weeks that I was carrying twins, because I needed to make sure it wasn't another ectopic situation. Armed with the knowledge it was twins and not another ectopic pregnancy, Tony decided we needed a larger car, and it would be a new one. He started searching for another minivan or an equivalent. You know, something to house our growing family. We had been looking at newer mini-vans, small SUVs, and larger SUVs. Tony was mainly looking for a car that could hold two car seats, a double wide stroller, one or two diaper bags, Kennedy, and his mother-in-law. Yes, my mother indicated she would be going with us to most of my doctor appointments and voluntold us she would need a place to sit so she could help with Kennedy and the twins. Hence the need for a bigger vehicle.

Alrighty then.

Fast forward to the sale of said shiny maroon Suburban to Sagel Anthony Simon and Laura Lorraine Simon. It was perfect. Eight passengers could fit quite comfortably. It had two captain's chairs up front, two benches that could seat three per bench, a huge cargo space that could easily hold a double-wide stroller, and barn doors for easy access.

That car was literally my dream come true. Of course, I wanted to drive it immediately and show it off. We had been driving a too small Infiniti M30, and I made Tony drive that ugly Astrovan because I didn't want to be seen in it. That van was awful: white exterior with black stripes and an ugly pointy front. Just not cute at all. Selfish? Absolutely. Did I care? Nope.

Don't judge me. I see you. Don't act like you have never made your husband do something you didn't want to do yourself. We all do it.

So, I was able to drive the shiny new car home. It was huge. To me. It was long. It sat high. Tony eventually got me a running board so I could climb into it like I was boarding the cab of an 18-wheeler. You do know a Suburban is classified as a truck. A truck. It took me about three years to figure out my car was a truck. I had never driven a car that big before. Tony convinced me with twins coming soon, I needed to get with the program and learn to drive this monstrosity. He said, "Laura, the front is short, the back is long." He really emphasized "front," "back," and "long."

Tony promised, "It really drives like a car because the front is short, and the back is long. You'll get the hang of it in no time."

And he was right. The Suburban drove like a car, and once you got the front in, the back was easy. And I loved driving it. We still have the maroon beauty, but it belongs to our son who was one of the reasons we bought it in the first place. I now drive a white Chevrolet Suburban and I'll never drive a car again. My next vehicle, I hope, will be a Range Rover. The big fat one. It's my dream car. Smile.

As I drove home, I must admit I was a little scared. While the car drove smoothly, it was just a lot of car. I should've known then God was about to help me out with the driving part. Not even two weeks later, the doctor put me on bed rest, so driving was completely out of the question. The day we bought the car was September 14, 1999. The twins were born December 14, 1999. Even though I wasn't supposed to, I think I drove the car only twice during that time. Yeah, I know, that's what I get for not driving the Astrovan.

Tony: Check.

God: Checkmate.

Since the anniversary was held the last two Sundays of September, Tony drove us to the church in the Astrovan. Ugh. Sigh. And I was getting bigger by the second. When we pulled up to the church and parked in the pastor's wife stall, quite a few members met us with excitement, and told us we needed a new car. At that time, they were eager to help us and wanted something nicer for the arrival of the two new babies!

THEM: Oh, Pastor and Sista Simon, y'all need a new car!

US: Wide eyes, slight smile, no verbal response.

Everyone was grinning and laughing and wishing us the best. But, oh, that would soon change.

The day of the celebration of our Pastor and Wife Anniversary/Appreciation arrived. The theme verse for the day was 1 Thessalonians 5:12-13 that says, "And now friends, we ask you to honor those leaders who work so hard for you, who have been given the responsibility of urging and guiding you along in your obedience. Overwhelm them with appreciation and love! Get along among yourselves, each of you doing your part."

The church was remarkable! They were kind, they were generous, and they truly showed their appreciation for our efforts in serving them. As I sat there in my beautifully decorated seat, I thought, *Surely, they won't be upset about the car. Look how excited they are for us! They're happy for us and they've given so much and so generously!* (And when I say much, I really mean much!)! We left the church that evening thinking this was the best anniversary/appreciation ever. But Tony wasn't swayed by their reactions. He said, "Laura, I'm still not driving that car up to the church for two weeks. Two Sundays. It's going to be a problem. Watch."

And he was right.

The second Sunday after the appreciation was October 2, 1999. I drove the car that day and I enjoyed it. Thank God because Tuesday, October 5, 1999, is when I was put on complete bed rest. I wouldn't drive the brand-new shiny Suburban again until February 2000. Another lesson learned for the PW.

Sigh.

Well, what else is there, Laura? Glad you asked.

Parishioners aren't the only folks who throw shade, hate on you, or pretend they're happy for you, but are secretly wondering how you did whatever you did. I want you to know throwing shade is an equal opportunity employer. The very people you think are in your corner, have your back, and love you dearly are the same ones who drag you down.

Step into my fishbowl, will you?

During the time leading up to the twins' birth, people said we should get a new car, but when we got the new car, all the Hatorade started pouring in under the guise of concern. Suddenly people were worried about our budget and wondering if Laura would be able to manage driving such a huge vehicle.

Yada, yada, yada.

Blah, blah, blah.

"Laura and Tony don't need that much of a car."

"Laura can't even drive that big ole car!"

"Laura and Tony could've gotten a smaller car."

"Laura and Tony don't need *that* much car." (Ever so slight word change).

"A minivan would've been just fine."

"A minivan would have sufficed."

"They say the car seats, stroller, and the mother-in-law won't fit in another smaller. I think they could have figured it out."

"Tony and Laura just showing off."

"Tony and Laura just got the car they wanted, regardless of their budget."

"Tony and Laura know they could-a just got a van."

"Well, a van carries lots of kids all the time.

WOW! Just wow. All Tony and I could do was blink our eyes in disbelief.

I quit trying to explain why we bought a Suburban. It was pointless. Those who knew what we were up against understood. Those who didn't want to understand, didn't want to even try seeing things our way. It was just that simple. I stopped talking about it. I just quit explaining, and gave them an eye piercing, eyebrow raising look. My stare was saying, "Just go sit down somewhere. You don't know my story."

In 2000 I was an elementary school teacher and I taught in a year-round school. Because it was year-round, we were placed on certain cycles: A, B, C or D. Cycle C was the closest to a traditional calendar with my time off being April, August, and December. During this season, my life was a total God-wink. He allowed me to start my new year in July, I was off in August, went back in September, then off again on total bedrest from October until my December delivery date. I was off with my babies and four-year-old until May— a total of six months! The twins were four and half months old when God winked at me again by having the principal move me to Cycle B. That meant I only taught fifth grade for the month of May. Of course, May had the Memorial Day holiday, so I was able to squeeze in a holiday in, work two more days with students, and then use one day to clean out my classroom and turn in grades. I'd be off the entire month of June and still get paid! Not to have to come back to teach until July 2000? Wow! Who does that? My God does that!

Why did I tell you all that? Because during that month, my mother could not watch the twins for three days. She and my dad went to a Grambling State University (our family's Alma Mater) event that was scheduled months prior, so she asked my PW Cousin if she would watch the five-month-old twins for three days: Wednesday, Thursday, and Friday. Ha!

"No problem," my cousin had said.

My mom wasn't as confident in her ability with two infants. "Are you sure? There's two of them."

"I'm sure. Plus, my mom will help me if need be."

"Okay," was my mom's tentative response, but she went along with the plan.

So Wednesday came, I went to work, and left Tony with the task of taking the twins to Cousin PW's house along with all their stuff and getting them settled.

Wait for it...

The first day she brought them back to our house for Tony so he wouldn't have to travel across town to pick them up.

(Cue laughter. Remember, everybody felt we didn't need a Suburban.)

When she got to our house, we went outside to find her car stuffed to capacity with the double-wide stroller, two car seats, the diaper bags, and of course, two babies. As she unfolded the stroller and dug out the diaper bags, and we lifted the twins out of her car and unfastened their car seats, she said, "Wow. They have *a lot* of stuff. I didn't realize it was so much, and did you see how it was stuffed in the back of my van?"

I tried not to say anything. I tried not to laugh. So, I simply said, "Now you see why we have a big car."

Pause.

"Thank you!" I yelled as she backed out of the driveway.

Pause.

"See you tomorrow!" *Chuckle here.* We waved goodbye.

The next day the same thing happened, but this time when she brought the twins home, she looked a little tired. After the car was unloaded of all the twin's *goods*, she said, "Man, they sure have a lot of *stuff*! I was finally able to *stuff* everything in the back of the van! How do you do it?"

I chuckled, "Yeah, that's why we have a Suburban."

I thanked her again for taking care of the kids, then added, "Just one more day!"

Her response was, "Oh, but they're good."

I just looked at her back out of the driveway.

But, oh, on Friday, I had to go to her house and pick up the twins and all their stuff. It seems PW Cousin was in the bed completely worn out. My aunt was waiting for me when I got to her house. Y'all, it took all of me to keep from getting on the ground and rolling all over in laughter. When I pulled up, my aunt was at the door waiting for me. The twins were all packed up and the stuff was ready to be loaded into my Suburban. You know, the one with the barn doors and ton of room in the back, two bench seats, and two captain's chairs. Yep, all my kids' stuff was lined up and ready to be loaded into the big ole car that I didn't need because a minivan would've been just fine.

"Where's Evangeline?" I asked.

My aunt replied, "Oh, she's upstairs laying down, child. Those twins wore her out, and I had to help."

"Oh really?"

"Girl, yeah. And all their stuff. Evangeline could barely fit all that stuff into her van. I see why y'all got that big ole car."

"Yeah. I told you all their stuff couldn't fit into a minivan. I told you we needed all that room...all of it. But nobody believed us."

"Oh yeah, Evangeline could barely fit the school kids *and* the twins *and* their car seats, *and* those diaper bags, *and that stroller*," she emphasized. "Girl, she can't believe, and *I* can't *believe* they have all that stuff, and it barely fit. Well actually, all that stuff doesn't fit. She crammed it all into her car and made it fit 'round all them kids and *their* stuff," she trailed off. "And they're so much work. I mean I kept kids for a living, but the amount of work was never like this," she finished.

"Well, there's two of them the exact same age at the same time. I tried to tell Evangeline how much work she was going to have to do was more than a notion. There are two babies at the same time! But it's over. My mom will be back next week, and Evangeline survived. Tell her thanks and get some rest!"

I got in the Suburban and backed out of the driveway without seeing poor, worn-out Van (short for Evangeline). Maybe I imagined it, but that big vehicle seemed to run exceptionally smoother that evening, as if she knew her work was justified. And I howled laughing all the way home as I drove my big old car with lots of room for baby stuff.

My mom called me when I got home to tell me the other side of the story, because my aunt didn't tell me everything. Seems as though the twins really wore PW Cousin out so much so, my aunt had to eat crow. She was the one who had proclaimed, "Oh, it'll be the same as keeping a lot of kids. I kept kids and this ain't nothin' 'cause it'll be just two babies. Plenty of people have had twins before. This ain't nothin' new, nothin' different. We can handle it."

Until they couldn't.

What is it about church folks—well, folks period? Why can't we just be honest? Why can't we just tell the truth—be real and be honest, or simply say "I don't know?"

Why must we make other people feel smaller to make ourselves feel bigger? I'm going to say that again because we do it. A lot. Why must we make other people feel smaller to make ourselves feel bigger? Do we ever stop to think about that?

Check yourself right now. Think about it right now. Ponder on it right now. Why? What makes you make others look small to boost yourself? And don't say you don't because you do. At some point we all have a moment. Admit it to God. Admit it to yourself. Then do something about it. Ask God to check your heart. Then ask Him what to do about it. He'll listen. He'll understand. He'll tell you what to do to fix it.

Your success is not my failure. And my success is not your failure. It took years for me to finally figure that out. We all have a place in God's kingdom—in the Body of Christ. Your gifts, your talents, your part will make room for you if you stop comparing yourself to other people and just let that "room" happen.

"In this way we are like the various parts of a human body. Each part gets its meaning from the body as a whole, not the other way around. The body we're talking about is Christ's body of chosen people. Each of us finds our meaning and function as a part of his body. But as a chopped-off finger or cut-off toe, we wouldn't amount to much, would we? So, since we find ourselves fashioned into all these excellently formed and marvelously functioning parts in Christ's body, let's just go ahead and be what we were made to be, without enviously or pridefully comparing ourselves with each other, or trying to be something we aren't." Romans 12:4-6.

I must segue here because I feel it in my spirit. I am so enthusiastic about this; I feel it in the depths of my soul.

I hear you asking, "What is it, Girl?"

The one thing I really want PW's, MW's, and women in leadership to get:

- Get rid of the mask(s).
- Stop the comparison(s).
- Get over yourself.

We tend to fake it 'til we make it. And that's what makes people give us the side-eye, the "Child please," and the "Who does she think she is" comments.

The other point I want to stress is that we don't have to react to all the shenanigans of the parishioners. They mean well sometimes. This is what I learned about 18 years ago: when talking to the church folks, just be real. They appreciate that. And it makes it so much easier on you. No more faking it. Just say what you need to say and temper it with a little bit a grace, and a little bit of mercy.

You'll see.

~

Questions, Reflections, and Things to Ponder

1. What do you need to admit? What's your whatchamacallit? What do *you* do?

2. How have you responded to the church members' Hatorade? Journal an example.

3. What was your takeaway about my situation?

    a. How would you have handled it? What did I do well? What didn't I do so well?

    b. How will you handle similar situations from now on?

4. Journal any thoughts or questions you want to discuss or ask me later.

5. Ask God to show you in what ways you might be faking it or wearing a mask? What does He want you to do about that? Journal your thoughts.

~

PRAYER

Father God, in the name of Jesus, help me trust You. I am Your vessel. I want to be more like Christ, and I want to stop comparing, stop avoiding, stop wearing masks, and I just want to be me. Show me how I can do that...with Your help. Give me the wisdom to handle the hard conversations and wisdom to handle the hard situations. Work on my mind, work in my heart, and adjust my attitude. Help me to deal with the Me in Me, help me to really SEE Me, and then help me to do something about it. I want to change, Oh God. Help me to see the best in everyone. In Jesus Name.

Chapter 9
Transformed and Classy: But I Still Cuss a Little

You know my wife said she doesn't understand why you and Pastor can never finish anything. Like you guys always start something but never finish it," said Brother Deacon, as if. As if he was so concerned and wanting to know why Pastor and I couldn't get our lives together. He said that to me. And I sat back in my captain's chair in my big white Suburban, took a sip, breathed out loud really hard and said a cuss word. Or maybe three of four in my head.

Then I said it to him.

It was like too late. The word had already come out of my mouth. And I didn't dare apologize because I didn't mean it – the apology that is. I meant to say the cuss word. And I meant to say it with an attitude and a sneer and a neck roll and an "Are you serious?" And an eyeroll and a pointed finger and an "Are you for real?"

You know what just chaps my hide? When church folks say funky and foul things to you and expect you not to say anything funky or foul back to them. I mean, they said it, so why can't I say it? My motto is this: if you can dish it out, then I can and will volley it back. And you better handle it like a boss. I mean, church folks want us to take what they say, and then we're supposed to just shrivel up and die, or at least get our feelings hurt and cry.

"Not so," says this pastor's wife. Like, help me. What's the difference? Tell me the difference between their rights and mine when it comes to opinions? Why come, not how come. Why come they can say whatever they want to say, and we can't? I know and say some of the same things church folks, the family, and the friends know and say.

I have learned to handle those situations and word wars much better now that I am in my thirtieth season of being a pastor's wife. But during those rookie years, yeah, folks who stepped to me wrong would've received an earful and would have taken a death-walk with me to the pastor's study. But, alas, I've changed. A lot!

Members feel their pastor and wife shouldn't say bad words. But we do. The pastor and wife shouldn't be smart alecks. But we are. We have gotten much better but shooting back a sharp quip is punctuated by a cuss word or two is in my husband's DNA; more about that later. I picked up my habit in college. I'm not proud about it, neither am I giving excuses. It is what it is. I own it. Now let me tell you about it.

Picture this: one of the old mothers of the church, Miss Hattie Mae Dunkin, had a tendency to say whatever came to her mind at any given moment on any given Sunday. She felt it was her right to tell you about yourself whenever the thought crossed her mind. Well, on one particular Sunday afternoon she felt the need to tell me about how mean and rude I was to a certain rude and snotty member. She told me just because I was the pastor's wife didn't mean it was right for me to snap at the other members even if they were wrong. She felt I should be the bigger person because I was the PW and just let it go. I should know better.

Well, ain't that the pot calling the kettle black.

I had reached my limit, and although I had already passed her pew with her still standing there, I stopped in the center aisle and slowly backed up. I never turned around; I just took about six or seven steps backward until I landed right next to her. I looked directly into her eyes and asked, "What did you say?"

She stuttered and said, "I didn't say anything, Sista Simon."

So, I looked at her and repeated to her what she had muttered to me. Then I loudly whispered, "I'm 'bout sick of you saying crap (you know in 1996 crap was the equivalent to sh*t) to me that's mean and ugly and not right just 'cause you think you can, and you think I won't say nothin' back to you. What would make you say what you said? What if I said to you, 'You're old, you're fat, and you're really ugly?'"

I waited a few seconds before I hissed, "And *that's* not being nice. I would never say that to you, but since you wanna go there, I'm going with ya. Stop saying crap like that to me and I won't say crap to you."

As I walked away, she muttered, "I'm gonna tell your husband."

"Go ahead and tell him," I said, flicking my right hand toward her and never turning back around.

I felt bad for a moment—for a very brief moment.

Then the feeling left when my husband called me back into the sanctuary to say Miss Hattie was offended by what I said to her. And on that day, I was able to vindicate myself. No, I wasn't. That day, the Lord vindicated me.

When I marched back into the sanctuary, I was hot as fish grease. I thought, *This woman has a lot of nerve!* When I stopped in front of my husband, eyes all ablaze, I asked him if Miss Hattie had told him what she said to me. Of course, she hadn't. So right in front of her I proceeded to tell him what she said to me. Then the narrative changed.

For the first time ever in a battle between wife and sheep, my pastor took up for me. What? Yes, my Pastor-Man-Husband-Baby-Daddy reprimanded his senior Mission Mothers' Board president. He told her ever so gently that she couldn't just say anything to his wife, or any of the other members of the church, and think someone wouldn't eventually get upset and just give it to her.

My eyes flew wide open in shock.

Her facial expression was priceless disbelief.

And I hear you saying as you identify with my rare victory, "Go on, Girl."

Now why was it such a shock that my guy had defended me? Because after he became the pastor, I was mostly in the wrong when it came to the members. They were great, and I was the cussing, fussing, nagging, oh-my-stars-always-complaining preacher's wife.

Those folks set me off on a regular.

That was back in the beginning when I was around 28 years old and didn't have a lot of wisdom, restraint, or compassion. Whatever people said to me, I said it back to them.

They'd say, "You think you're so much, and know so much."

I'd say, "I am, and I do."

They'd say, "You think you're so smart, and we're stupid."

I'd say, "You said that, I didn't."

They'd say, "Oh."

I'd echo, "Oh, oh, oh, oh. Right back at 'ya."

Those first years were very dark and challenging times. I pretty much damned them to hell.

A lot.

Before my husband planted our current church, he pastored another church in our city that was and still is full of members we'd grown up with. That was hard. Those folks felt it was okay to say whatever they wanted to say to us and we'd be expected to either be okay with it, or not be okay with it but say nothing back.

They were wrong.

Back then I'd respond with just what they gave me. Not all words were cuss words, but I used some not-so-nice words like dumb, stupid, or ignorant. Only thing was I'd add a salty "ass" at the end, and say, "You dumb-a--, you stupid-a--, or you ignorant-a--.

Don't judge me.

If you're thinking, *Wow, she said that?* I just want you to remember: your sin might not be my sin, but you do have a sin.

Take a sip. We will talk more about that in the "How Fake Do You Want Me To Be" chapter.

Here's the thing, I have a cussing habit that I still

talk to God about. This is one of the conversations I have with God on a regular basis:

"God, now I know I told You I would do better, but dang it, (insert name) has straight pissed me off.

You're reading in disbelief, "Did she say 'pissed off' to God?"

"God, that blank-iti-blank cut me off. Jesus, I did not mean to call her that, but...

Now back to the skank who I spoke to sideways in the first place, "What the bleep did you say? What the bleepity-bleep did you mean?

In the ear of my heart came the whisper from God, "Didn't you tell me you wanted to stop cussing? Didn't you tell me you were going to not say that word? Laura!"

"Que lastima!" (Translation: What a pity.) "Aye."

Look, I hear you, and I see your eyes all big. And I do pray and then I pray some more. It's not like I don't make the effort to do better. I did and I do. But it's just so easy to slip back into old habits. And I know the verse by heart, "Therefore if any man be in Christ, he is a new creature; old things are passed away; behold, all things are become new." 2 Cor. 5:17 KJV

There are many days when I go without saying one cuss word. Then there are days I simply stub my toe, get cut off by another driver, yell at my kids, or get into a verbal joust with my husband that sends me on a tangent. This fact amazes even me. At any given time, if it's something I'm passionate about, if there's even a remote chance that emotions are involved, one of those words may escape my lips.

My friend Sonya moved to Texas and started telling me about her pastor's wife. She said, "Laura, our Pastor

Lorraine is a cusser...and will tell you that in a minute."

My eyes got big as saucers just as I imagine yours are right now. I replied, "Are you serious?"

Sonya said, "Oh yes. She gets on the stage and tells us how saved she is, but she has a potty mouth. Says she's working on it—continually."

Well. Well. Well. And that right there piqued my interest, so I said, "And what do the ladies... what do the members say?"

Sonya replied, "We all know. And we all have something we're working on, so we really don't say anything to her about it. It's like, that's our Pastor and she's working on some things."

And that was that.

Her sharing the stories about her Texas PW was illuminating and freeing. It's not what she said, well, yeah it was, but to me, to my soul, to my spirit, to my cussing tongue, it was an "aha" moment. Not that cussing is right, not *that* at all. It was the fact that someone else, another PW, had an issue like mine. And that's one of the reasons I appreciate Pastor Lorraine so much. Her sin is out in the open and she makes no bones about it. She owns it, and she lets people know she's still working on it. And that's me. It pains me when some of the words tumble out of my mouth and folks be looking at me like, "Girl, did you hear the PW?" Their eyes are all incredulously wide and stuff. And I swiftly look at them all side-eyed and ask, "So you never cuss?"

Listen, I understand my position. I also understand who I am. It's not always pretty, but I refuse to be fake. I am good for asking our church folks if "unflowery" words sometimes fall from their lips. When they respond with a great big, "YES," I say, "Well, that applies to my life as well."

Here's the thing Sister-Friend-Girl, we are all working on something, and if you admit it, you are, too, I just choose to say out loud what I'm struggling with. When I do that, not bragging or saying this is right for you, but it could be. I'm just saying, being honest about my struggles keeps me humble. It keeps me from having to remember what I may have said or lied about saying, and it also shows others that I am human, and not so holy that I'm no earthly good.

Now don't get it twisted, I am not saying it's okay to just cuss out loud in front of the "people," but I am saying if you find yourself in their company and it comes out, just get ready. Be honest. Be up front. Be authentic. People usually understand unless they've forgotten about their own tendencies. And if they do forget, let 'em. It's okay. Don't go into defense mode. Simply explain your truth in a First Thessalonians 5 kind of way and keep it pushin'. If you stay too long trying to explain, or justify, or get your point across as to why, just stop; cut it out. It's not worth it.

"They" are already looking at you crazy and your honesty is not going to make them change their minds until they're good and ready to. Whatever the members think of you now is what they will think of you now. Only God can change that narrative. So, you do you Boo. Ask God to change you and help *you*.

Why do I say that? Because it's part of our fishbowl life. When you're sincere and mean it, God honors that. I know He does. And you trying to change someone else's judgmental spirit when they have a ton of their own crap just makes you even crazier. Don't be offended. All PWs are a little crazy to a certain extent. You are in this group. Own it.

So how do we deal with this? If any man be in Christ, he or she is a new creation. I'm here again. Every time I say something off that I know I shouldn't say, I recall this verse. It helps keep me in check. It reminds me and you to give everything to God and He will make your path straight – if you want Him to.

~

What if you don't cuss, but you say not nice things? What if you look side-eyed at the folks or roll your eyes at them? What if you're rude, or have the tendency to speak harshly to people? You still have to turn it over to God and ask for His guidance and His help. 1 Peter 5:6-7 in the Phillips New Testament translation of the Bible says, "So, humble yourselves under God's strong hand, and in his own good time he will lift you up. You can throw the whole weight of your anxieties upon him, for you are his personal concern."

Let me tell you what happened to me right before the pandemic. No, I didn't cuss out said member, but boy oh boy, there was some major damage that had to be cleaned up by the angels; and, if I must say so myself, my angels did a phenomenal job. I can be dismissive. Yes, I said it out loud, and yes, I'm owning up to it. Some members just work my nerves and I have a hard time finding the best in them. I don't cuss at them, but I have a tendency of being smart-alecky and calling them stupid. Now stupid is the five-year old's equivalent to dumb donkey, King James Version, and if my little kids hear it, they tell me about it. "Don't say stupid, Sista Simon. That's a bad word."

Alright, so said member comes up to me and just says an asinine remark and is waiting for me to respond with something nice but witty. Nope. Not today. It's our appreciation service and I'm surrounded by lots of nice church members, not so nice nosey church members, and other guest church members who, too, are nice and not so nice. You know the ones. They're hanging around to see what they can see and hear and don't mean you a bit of good. Yes, those members. They're what we call Nice-Nasty. Anyway, my church member said something about what I was wearing, and the comment wasn't a compliment. Well, she was and still is old (not wise, just old), and it probably was a compliment in her mind, or maybe not, but it most certainly was not a compliment in mine. So, after she said the crazy statement, I said, "You are just so stupid." (Right here, insert crazy look on my face.)

In my mind I thought, *Oh, my stars, did I say that out loud? Holy crap, Laura, did you just say that out loud?*

I looked down, waiting for a response, muttering in my mind, *Yes, yes, you said that out loud! Oh my gosh! Oh my gosh! Tony's going to kill me; Tony's going to kill me!* And as I stood there in sheer panic mode asking God to please help me get out of this, said church member leans into me and said, "Pardon me dear, what did you say?"

Oh! Talk about relief! I started jumping up and down doing the happy dance and cheerfully replied, "Oh Sister Smith, I was just saying how good it was seeing you tonight. I know you've been missing in action lately."

Whoo! Praise the Lord I dodged *that* bullet! In a

nano second God had dispatched the angels and I literally saw them fanning my words away. Fanning away me calling that woman stupid! Oh, talk about a giddy PW! That was me!

Here's the issue: we think a lot of things and if we're not careful, those things will come out of our mouths. I thanked God on that night! I thanked Him for the service, for the people, and for the angels He sent that saved me from certain verbal death at the hands of Tony Simon.

Work on your mouth. Work on your thoughts. Work on you. My version of 1 Thessalonians 5:14-15 says, "And when they get on your last nerve, see them as God sees them, through the eyes of Jesus. See the best in them and do your best to bring it out. Even though the members can and will say some horrific things, it is still our duty to remember they are God's children, too. And when they do, say crazy-ish things, we need to see the best in them.

"Are you serious?" you ask.

Yes, and while you're at it, show those church members love, offer mercy, and extend grace; you would want mercy and grace extended to you, right? Plus, if you're reading this book and are interested in making the needed changes, God has already extended more grace and mercy than you could ever deserve. Think about that.

I'll wait.

Take a sip.

~

Reflections, Things to Ponder & Prayer

1. What constitutes bad words or a bad word?

2. Do you agree that a bad word can be a look, an attitude, or something else?

3. Journal about your "bad word." What is God saying to you about it?

4. How can you make changes?

PRAYER

Father in the name of Jesus, help me, oh God, with my words, my thoughts, and my actions. Let me know how to say things, what to say, and when to say it. Please God, allow me to see the best in everyone. Please Jesus, help me to extend peace, love, and grace to all I meet. Teach me how to choose my words wisely and be a better example. Thank You God, in Jesus Name.

Chapter 10
How Fake Do You Want Me to Be?

S is, just pray about it. God will make it all right."
"Yeah, Sis, just pray about it."
"You're worrying about nothing. It'll be fine."

I responded, "Okay, but I still want prayer."

This is the kind of dialogue that makes people look at PWs either like they're fake, or like everything's fine. Well, sometimes everything is *not* fine. It's okay to not be okay. And it's okay to talk about it. We lose more of our sisters to the craziness of trying just being tired or a little stressed. No, depression is real. And depression can display as stress, anxiety, physical fatigue, or feeling overwhelmed. We need to address the myriad of issues pastor's wives and women in general face and battle on a daily basis.

Yes, God can make everything all right, and yes, God can help you through anything. But sometimes we must address the issues at hand with a mental health professional like a therapist, a counselor, a psychologist, or a life coach. There are times we need to chat it out, and I'm one of the PWs who firmly believes in the power of prayer and therapy. The above conversation came in the 2020 Year of the Pandemic. It's not like we're out of the pandemic, but we're out of the year 2020.

Let's go back in time, shall we?

I've always been a person who says what is on my mind. Again, not that I want to offend anyone, but in my opinion, it's just so much easier to tell the truth than make up a lie. or hide your true feelings about things that bother you.

I belong to several pastor's wives' groups that started in 2020. We were stuck in the house with our pastor-husbands, PKs, in-laws, out-laws, and pets, and we worked from home. All those pieces rumbling around together was a deadly combination. Deadly as in death to one's nerves, death to the kids leaving the house going to school or *somewhere,* and death to romance (or not because some of y'all got busy and had pandemic babies). It was death to the husband not going to the church, and death to any type of me-time. Everybody was in the house. So, we joined pastors' wives' groups, and any other groups that would help us have, keep, or bring back our sanity.

"Those of us who are strong and able in the faith need to step in and lend a hand to those who falter, and not just do what is most convenient for us. Strength is for service, not status. Each one of us needs to look after the good of the people around us, asking questions, "How can I help?" Romans 15:2 This verse was the foundation for the groups. Those who were strong started groups that helped PWs and women in ministry cope with their families. There was only one teeny weeny problem: some of us weren't being real.

We weren't real about our lives, our spouses, our children, or our churches. Heck, we weren't even real about ourselves. Fakeness at its finest. Now don't get me wrong, there were and still are groups that are authentic, and the ladies could and still can be themselves because those real groups were and still are safe environments.

But then there were those groups that perpetuated fakeness. Those were the ones in which everyone was addressed as "Sis."

Ugh.

Sigh.

Stop it.

Now is not the time to pretend you don't know what I'm talking about. You know and I know everybody ain't "Sis" material. Some folks can call other people "Sis" genuinely from the heart. You feel it, and you know the greeting is sincere. Then there's the other "Sis," and you don't feel it, you know the greeting is fake, and you know it ain't sincere.

Whoo! And so that's when I posed the question to my husband, "How fake do I have to be?" I told Tony I couldn't take it. I said if another woman calls me Sis I'm going to scream. And I didn't want another woman telling me to just pray and every problem would, "Poof, be gone!" as if God was this cosmic genie in a bottle who magically granted wishes.

Yeah.

No.

Dealing with women who were afraid to be real reminded me of when I was at Starbucks with the Stepford Church Wives. I had demanded, "Will somebody please tell the truth!" My husband was getting on my last nerve, my kids were driving me nuts, I was trying to navigate Zoom meetings for work and church, and then I was my son's hall monitor for Home Zoom School. I was a mess, and the holy PWs were saying, "It'll be alright, Sis." What? What will be alright? When it got to be too much, I just reverted back to my old self and said whatever came to my mind.

We cannot help anyone by not telling the truth. We cannot get better, recover, or heal while sharing half-truths. And so, this one group allowed me to say, "I hate my husband. I hate my kids. And right now, I hate the church folks." Ah, it was like screaming, "Freedom!" Think of an opera singer singing, "Freedom!" I could be my true self, and share my true words, and be vulnerable and bare my soul without judgment. No more faking fine here! That was a 2019 theme from a women's conference I did in New Jersey: No More Faking Fine.

Authenticity. That's what we shared in PWDW (Pastors' Wives Do Workout). Our leader, Cledra, modeled how to show up authentically in the pandemic life, but more importantly, how to show up authentically in the game of life. There was no room for the fake stuff. Anything made to appear other than real is actually and obviously counterfeit. That's the elementary definition, and we were encouraged to be real, to be honest, and to be authentic.

In 2020, the only rule in PWDW was that we had to post at least one workout a week in the group feed, and it could be a text message, a picture, or both. The optional Zoom call happened once a week, and since Cledra was on the East coast, the time of the call for me was early in the morning, and I am *not* an early morning person. During many a 7am Friday morning call, my camera was either off or I was sitting there in the bed looking like I just woke up, because I had.

One morning I was literally laying in the bed, with my head still on the pillow, hair wrapped up in my scarf, sleep crust in the crevices of both eyes, and hubby snoring to my left. But I was there, I was present, and although my eyes were still closed, Cledra called on me to pray. We took turns. Some days I was asked to pray us "in" or pray us "out." *Insert big eyed look.* And then I'd have to wake up fast and in a hurry.

Help soon came from another West coast PW, Meredith. Meredith is from another generation. Another generation that is not my generation but is the other generation that wakes up early. She was my help! Meredith started sending me a 6:45am text that woke me up by 6:58am so I could make it on the call on time without looking so sleepy.

I'm sharing this with you because this is as real as it gets. I couldn't fake it. I had a hard time getting up on Friday's that early. And guess what? Not only did the ladies and Cledra appreciate my transparency, but telling that truth was a part of what made me *me*. Although I tried once to look like I was up and ready to go, it just proved too much for me to fake it. I became known in not just this group, but in all the groups I'm in as the PW who doesn't shy away from anything. She doesn't hide her weaknesses in order to appear good, perfect, or problem free.

It's not good to pretend you're something that you're not. That pretense always comes back to haunt you. Again, during 2020, my whole attitude was under reconstruction. I joined pastor's wives' groups, as well as writer's groups, and any other groups I thought would help me through the pandemic.

However, I had been tussling with God since 2008 about the writing of this book. He had put it in my heart to talk about the life and times of women in leadership, especially the pastor's wife.

God said, "You know about the life, and I want you to share what you've learned."

And I responded, "Who wants to hear from me? I'm such the rebel."

But God kept on pressing, so here we are. Now don't get me wrong, I try my best to obey God on a regular, however, some days I'm not the most obedient daughter.

With so much time on my hands in 2020 I attended quite a few virtual writer's conferences, but the 2020 She Writes for Him Conference would be life altering. The conference was the best one I had ever attended even though it was virtual. I literally sat in my big chair in the living-room-turned-church-turned-studio and watched the ladies that made up Redemption Press for three solid days. All the information was mind blowing, and at the end of the third day, Redemption's owner announced that the She Writes for Him (SWFH) Conference was offering a follow-up bootcamp for writers.

I jumped at the chance to attend the bootcamp because I thought, "If the conference was this good, then an intimate time with other writers would be phenomenal." So, I registered for the bootcamp and called my agent to tell her what I'd done. She thought it was a great idea and encouraged me to learn as much as I could from the other writers so I could move forward with my writing efforts.

After I registered, I was prompted to film and share an introduction video telling a little bit about myself, my writing journey, and what I wanted to gain from the experience. If I had done the video right then and there, I would've been the first participant to complete the task. However, I did my usual and procrastinated. I waited a few days and watched all the other women share their stories. As the recording deadline quickly approached, I found myself hesitating to record a video. You see, because I waited so long, I was able to watch all the participating writers' videos, and to my disappointment, there were no other women of color. It looked like I would be the only one. And that didn't sit with well with me at all.

Oh no. Oh no, no, no. I will not be the only Black woman in this bootcamp. I'll just stand on the outside, look in, and not participate.

But God.

Big sigh.

He had a little chat with me and told me I couldn't back out. I would make the video, and I would show up and participate in the bootcamp.

Alrighty then.

Now this is where everything about being fake is put on full display. I participated in all the activities in the bootcamp, and I even had a bootcamp buddy named Tracey. She was my number one encourager and told me the book I was writing (the book you're now holding) would help so many women who were afraid to show their true selves.

Tracey and I talked about everything, even our personal lives, and how racism was dividing the church and believers. When the death of George Floyd played out in the media, she and I had a hard conversation. At some point, I shared with her my challenges with raising two boys in Orange County, California. I told her how we were the only Black family in our neighborhood and my boys were pulled over often by the police for no reason at all.

Also, during that time, the Black Lives Matter movement was championing the cause of racial injustice heavily on television, in the streets, and on social media. One of memes pushed on Facebook and Instagram was "My Sons Matter" and because I have two sons, I posted the meme on my page. Most people were encouraging and responded with positive words, but there was one woman who happily posted an ignorant response. She answered me by name and said she had two boys and their lives mattered too. And then a fellow bootcamp buddy (not Tracey) "hearted" her. And I lost it. I mean, I was livid, as in over the top. I wanted to blast her, but God wouldn't let me. He wouldn't even let me type a response back to her. God wouldn't allow me to type anything.

Not one thing.

The more I typed, the more God said, "Erase that. You're not posting one word."

And so, I didn't. But man, oh man, I received a ton of smack talk from my friends and family. They were saying things like:

"When are you gonna respond?"

"Who is this woman?"

"Are her sons Black?"

"What nerve. Are you not gonna answer her?"

And on it went. Finally, a childhood friend called

me and asked, "So you're telling me God won't let you respond?"

"Right, God said not to."

"Then I will. He ain't told me nothin.'"

She hung up and proceeded to try. And try. And try again. After the fifth time of typing and finally being able to post a long, nasty, petty response to this woman, she couldn't find the original post! The post had simply disappeared!

I laughed when she called me back with her story of how she had tried and tried and tried and then when she thought she had posted something, she couldn't find the original, she said, "Apparently God doesn't want me to post anything either. I'm so mad."

"Don't be mad, Girl," I told her. "There's a lesson in this."

So, I looked the woman up on Facebook and found that she was and still is a *Karen*, and her boys are totally White. Listen, I don't care about her being White. What I do care about is she didn't and still doesn't get my story.

You see, I was sharing my experience about my sons. Lots of people who are not Black have either never heard of or simply do not believe the level of racism against African Americans that still exists in America. I shared the meme that said, "Black sons matter," because their lives were not held in high esteem, and they were not respected. The appropriate response would have been, "You're right, Laura, we're with you. We finally understand it's long about time your sons' lives matter in this country." For a White person to follow our declaration with, "My sons matter too," is like stopping the firetruck at your house to do prevention when the engine needs to douse the fire that's burning at my house. Society already treats your sons with respect; that fact does not need to be declared. Our sons are looked over, harassed unfairly, treated brutally, and murdered unnecessarily.

This is what I mean when I say we must have the hard conversations but share compassion and show empathy when having the discussions. There is no time like the present to remove the barriers, stop with the no-truths or half-truths, let go of the fake-I'm-fine, and be the women God has called us to be. When you're a pretender, eventually the pretender in you is found out. Stop it. Just stop it.

Romans 12:6 says, "Just go ahead and be what we were made to be, without enviously or pridefully comparing ourselves with each other, or trying to be something we aren't." And Romans 12:9 sums up the idea saying, "Love from the center of who you are; don't fake it."

What the pandemic of 2020 and the She Writes for Him Bootcamp did was allow a God-wink. God winked at every one of us who allowed Him to. He allowed me to be seen, and He woke those White sisters who allowed Him to come in and wake them up! I can't say they all received a "woke moment," but those who wanted to wake up, did. What the enemy meant for evil; God used for good. According to Paul, God wants us to keep our eyes open. "If you're called to give aid to people in distress, keep your eye open and be quick to respond; if you work with the disadvantaged, don't let yourself get irritated with them or depressed by them. Keep a smile on your face" Romans 12:7-8.

My sisters were in distress and needed their eyes

opened. Instead of being selfish, Paul wrote we should be quick to respond. My sisters were disadvantaged when it came to knowing my struggle. It wasn't the time for me to get irritated, angry, or depressed by them. I should have kept a smile on my face.

But I was so turned off by the SWFH conference woman, and the bootcamp person who hearted her ridiculous response that I vowed to keep my mouth shut, not participate in any more activities, and planned to have my camera turned off on the next Zoom session. And I sat there in front of my laptop for a good 15 minutes before it was time to go on and argued with God. I also argued with my husband.

"I am not going on that stupid Zoom with all those White women." I was adamant.

God was calm. "Yes. Yes, you are."

"No. No I'm not."

Tony looked at me like I was crazy. "What are you in there muttering about?"

"I'm not going on the Zoom today. I'm not showing up with all these White women! Do you know one of the bootcampers had the nerve to "heart" that crazy bigoted woman's response?"

God was not taking my "no" for an answer. "And what a lesson you'll teach. Get on the Zoom. Now!"

Tony wasn't taking my "no" for an answer either. "Girl, get on that Zoom and talk to them. Tell them."

"I don't want to."

God kept up His pressure. "I don't care. Turn the camera on and *you will* show up and *you will* participate.

I logged in, turned on the camera, and participated.

That was the beginning of my hard conversations

with women, with people, with sisters who didn't look like me. I wasn't allowed to be fake or fake-fine. God made sure I had no choice but to be obedient to Him and do exactly what He said.

And that's when it happened. From the hard conversations, a book was born. Something I never imagined. Here's what Redemption's owner wrote:

> "It was the first week of June, so the death of George Floyd was front and center in the news and at the top of the minds of many. We were wrapping up one of the training calls for the She Writes for Him Bootcamp. Thirty-plus women, excited to learn how to tell their stories, were crammed onto a Zoom call. Cynthia, from our She Writes team, directed her question to the lone Black sister in the group.
>
> "So, Laura, with everything going on, how are *you* doing?"

Long pause.

> "Well, it's been hard. I struggle to find words to express my emotions. I'm crying a lot."
>
> That began a raw conversation with our sister in Christ who opened our eyes to so many things."

Had I not listened to the voice of God, *She Writes for Him Black Voices of Wisdom* never would have come to fruition. That day I told my White sisters to ask me the hard questions and have the hard conversations with me. No more faking fine and skirting the issue of racism in the religious arena. I was already doing it in the secular world, now it was time to pull the cover off the eyes of the believers. The only way we would come to a better understanding of each other was to talk about it. Out of that bootcamp conversation came a beautiful book written by 21 black women sharing their stories of racism and how God stood with them, stood by them, and carried them through.

When your truth isn't spoken, you miss out on opportunities to share the hard stories and have the hard conversations. "No Room in the City" is the thirteenth chapter in the *She Writes for Him Black Voices of Wisdom* book. Had I hidden my raw feelings about my truth, that book probably wouldn't be here.

Stop pretending. Stop faking fine. Stop being someone you're not.

Show the real you.

Show up as the real you: weaknesses, strengths, flaws, your good, your bad, and your ugly. Show it all, and when you do, temper it with grace, temper it with love, and temper it with mercy. People receive you differently when you're real.

God can use an authentic you, but He can't use a counterfeit you.

~

Questions, Reflections, Things to Ponder

1. Who are you? What makes you happy? What makes you sad? What sends you to the ledge? What makes you want to jump? Journal your answers to these questions.

2. When you pretend—when you fake-fine—again what's your trigger? What makes

you pretend? What makes you hide behind the mask(s)? Do you even know?

3. Ask God to help you see your fakeness. Then ask Him to help you understand what makes you fake it. Journal all of your true feelings and then pray about it all.

4. After praying about it, ask yourself and ask God if you're part of the problem and how you can become part of the solution.

5. Read Romans 12 once all the way through, then focus on verses 4-21. Pray over the passage and then apply it to some of the situations discussed in this chapter. Write down your thoughts, feelings, or takeaways. I believe you'll have a different perspective.

PRAYER

Father God, I ask You to help me take a good look at myself. Show me where I'm fake, where I put on airs, where I think more highly of myself than I ought to. Help me see myself and others the way You see us, through the eyes of Jesus. Let me see where pride has blinded me to my flaws and strengthen me to be more like You. Help me to see the best in myself and the best in others. And then God help me to stop comparing myself to others or trying to be something I am not. Help me to not hit back but discover the beauty in everyone. Help me not to be stuck-up. Let me make friends with nobodies and not try to be the great somebody. Let me love deeply and be a genuine friend. In Jesus Name.

LAURA SIMON

Chapter 11
But I Didn't Do Anything

O h, my stars! Can we just end Bible study already?" I shouted from the second row.

"No!" Tony shouted back from behind the podium. "I don't care what you want," he continued. So, I sat back down and folded my arms. That Sally got me again.

Under my breath I muttered, "I'm so sick and tired of her. I wish she would just leave the church." I whispered loud enough for her to hear. "She just causes drama all the time."

Then the other members at Bible study started chiming in. "That Sally is always saying or doing something to tick people off, then she acts like she didn't do anything," said the Chairman of the Deacon Board.

"Yep, and that's why you should tell the pastor," I said. "He'll listen to you."

And so, I sat there with my arms folded and tried to keep my mouth shut. If I had another outburst, Pastor-Man was going to really let me have an ear full when I got home.

And so, Sally started talking again and she has such an annoying voice that you'd rather listen to fingernails on a chalkboard. She's always looking down her nose at someone, or trying to chastise the youth and young adults, or saying crazy stuff to the media guy, or being snippety with my mom who's even more vocal than I am. What gets me with Sally Member is she can dish it out, but she can't take it; and boy can my mom dish it out.

It all started when we were visiting a church across town. One of the guest soloists got to singing and singing and singing until she just wore the audience out. Okay, so it was my mother she wore out. Anyway, when the soloist finally stopped singing, she walked off the stage and straight into my mother who told her in no uncertain terms that she sang the song entirely too long for the program. Mom instructed her that she needed to be considerate of her audience. But my mother wasn't finished with that. She went a bit further and told the soloist that she had cut into the preacher's preaching time, which was rude and unfair, and now the audience would suffer because he would have to cut his sermon short. Mom concluded by telling her the next time a church invited her to sing, she should think about how long she should sing, and make sure next time she didn't go over her time limit.

The bad part was my mother reprimanded the woman at the front of the church, kind of off to the side. Now neither the congregation nor I witnessed my mom taking the soloist to the side, but of course Miss Sally did. And Miss Sally figured she would tell my mother a thing or two without any consequences. After all, the soloist was Miss Sally's friend, and my mother was wrong.

Oh my, but Miss Sally was wrong, too. She let her anger fester for at least two years before saying something to my mother and she didn't take my mother to the side when she let it all out. She berated my mom in public. Now when my mother's feelings were hurt, she lashed out and gave Miss Sally a run for her money, so Miss Sally then tattled to Pastor-Man.

"But Pastor," Miss Sally whined, "I didn't do anything. I was just telling her how wrong she was."

My follow-up question to Miss Sally was, "What about you?"

Again, I didn't have to worry about Miss Sally. She had to contend with the other church members about the way she talked to Mother Rhetta. Reaping what you sow is no laughing matter. And reaping what you sow doesn't take long either.

I'm going to say it again: Miss Sally can dish it out, but Miss Sally can't take it when the tables are turned. She's the type of member who throws a rock and hides her hand, then pretends she didn't do anything. The first couple of times she did it, Pastor-Man didn't realize what was happening, but later, he saw it for himself and realized Miss Sally was a bitter woman who had never fully recovered from her own trauma. When we don't work on ourselves with Jesus and therapy, there's a strong possibility that we might not ever heal. That must be a miserable feeling.

Well, how ironic that after she raised all that hell about my mother, she would go outside and act a fool with Ron, our media guy. We were passing out dessert after service, and she came outside to the table where

Ron and I were standing. Although I am the pastor's wife, and she doesn't much care for me, my kids, or my mother, I guess she was aggravated because she had gotten nowhere with her complaints about my mom. So, she took it out on Ron. (She very well knew she wasn't going to take it out on me. I was waiting for her, and she already knew I could be just as petty as she). She was very rude, very loud, and very not Christ-like when addressing Ron.

Ron was trying to help her, but she wouldn't hear of it. She went into obnoxious mode, and he quickly said, "Now Miss Sally, didn't we just get out of church? You're talking all crazy to me and it seems like you wouldn't do that since we *did* just get out of church. Besides, I ain't done nothing to you," and he started chuckling, which further irritated her.

She was so mad at Ron that she yelled back, "I don't care if we did just get out of church, you were being rude to me, and I'm not going to take it!"

"Now wait a minute, Miss Sally, you said I was rude to *you*?" He was laughing as he turned to look at me, but I could tell he was getting angry with her, so he turned to me and said, "First Lady, was I rude to her? I mean she was the one yelling at me and I was just offering her a piece of cake."

I happily answered, "You were not rude. It appears she's still upset about my mother and what happened inside the church."

With that, she stomped to her car. "Bye Miss Sally," Ron called after her, "Hope you feel better." Then he turned to me and said, "That Miss Sally is awful." I agreed.

But there's more. Miss Sally is one of those

members who is a bully. A straight antagonist. She's the type of member who picks at the young people and then gets offended when they come for her, and the other adult members don't say a word. Or she's really hot when the other adult members defend the youth against her and then proceed to light her up! But of course, Miss Sally doesn't see it that way. She feels she doesn't do anything and can't figure out why the children look at her all side eyed. I know why they do, and if I could fire her up myself, I would, but then I'd have to hear from the Pastor-Man about my behavior, so I let the other parishioners take the lead.

On another Sunday, Miss Sally decided she was going to have a stare down contest with the youth and young adults; my children being in the young adult category. For whatever reason, Miss Sally kept turning around during service shushing the kids in the two rows behind her. Little did she know the whispering wasn't coming from the youth but from the grown adults one row ahead of them. I know because I was texting my kids to be quiet, when I saw it wasn't them.

"My bad," I whispered to them, and turned around.

Anyway, Miss Sally kept turning around giving the kids the evil eye and making harsh sounds from across the room. Meanwhile, I was getting hotter by the second, but God stepped in and sent an angel by way of Auntie-Cousin-Member who got up and moved to the back row to sit with the young folks. Still, Miss Sally kept on mad dogging the kids, shushing them, mouthing, "Be quiet," and just doing too much.

Finally, the young people couldn't stand it anymore, and they all got up and walked outside. Now before they got up, Miss Sally said something crazy to the effect of stop talking or you're talking too much, or I know it's you talking, or something like that. My teenage daughter told her it wasn't them and to leave them alone. And, oh, Miss Sally really got mad. But what she didn't count on was Auntie-Cousin-Member getting up, going outside after the kids, and then walking them back into the sanctuary so they could finish hearing the sermon.

Pastor-Man was talking to them about young people's topics, and then he directed his words to Miss Sally. He said, "Enough is enough. Stop provoking kids because you'll run them away from church."

So, Miss Sally turned around and looked at my husband as if she hadn't done a thing. She tried to look all innocent and I was looking at Miss Sally and my husband thinking, *You've got to be kidding me. Surely, you're not falling for her act, are you?*

This time when she turned around again Auntie-Cousin was waiting for her with, "Girl please," and told her to stop bothering the kids and to turn around and stop talking.

I almost hollered. Witnessing that exchange made my *day*! Member-Auntie-Cousin handled Miss Sally so, that I just turned around, sat back, and put my head down to keep from laughing. But I couldn't stop. I laughed so hard I almost hurt myself. Miss Sally had met her match. After church she *tried* to say something to the pastor, but Pastor-Man wasn't having it. He said, "Miss Sally, somebody has to be mature enough to be quiet. It's not always the children. Sometimes it's us."

And I just said, "Humph," and walked away.

Or there was the time when I went off on Miss Sally. Like I totally lost it in front of the Bible study class. She was running her mouth, saying crazy stuff as usual and I just couldn't take it anymore. We were on Facebook live and in person. The people online started typing in comments.

"Why doesn't Miss Sally be quiet?"

"Why doesn't Miss Sally stop talking?"

"Why is Miss Sally even asking that?"

The comments continued, so I said something petty, and my husband then got on me, so I didn't say anything for the rest of the Bible study. But oh, when we got in his truck, I started screaming, "I am sick and tired of Miss Sally and all her $%*! and you're always taking up for her raggedy @$%. Tonight, she was wrong, and you know it! And I was wrong for calling her out, but I'm not apologizing. I'm sick of her!"

And she heard me. Even with the windows rolled up.

I did not care, and I told my husband, I did not care.

When we pulled up in the driveway at home, I hopped out of the car immediately and dialed my cousins who were listening to the Facebook Live. They said, "What was going on with Miss Sally tonight? She was on one! And what made you go off on her?"

I said, "That doggone Tony Simon. He's always taking up for her, and I couldn't take it anymore, so I yelled at her and told him to end the class. I know I shouldn't have let her get the best of me, but she just irks the hell out of me."

Then my prayer warrior cousin says, "Now Laura, just calm down and let's pray."

I responded, "Evangeline, I don't want to pray. Gwen, tell her I don't want to pray. Save it for someone who cares, and right now I don't care. Same thing I told

Tony, I'm sick of him taking up for her when he knows she's dead wrong, so, no, don't pray for me."

Prayer Warrior knew me. "Ok. That's fair."

Auntie-Cousin's-Prayer-Warrior sister said, "We get it."

Then the devil added his two cents. Miss Sally's number pops up on my phone while I'm walking and talking to my cousins. I hurriedly click over because I want to hear what Miss Sally has to say.

I answer, "Hello," pause, then again, I said, "Hello."

Again, there is still no voice from the other end of the phone. I shout, "Hello."

Miss Sally finally said something. "Hello…"

I interrupted and said, "You called me?"

"No, it dialed on its own when I hit a bump."

So, I played along with her, "Ok. Goodbye."

Then I clicked over to my cousins and said, "She said the seat dialed me when she hit a bump."

My cousin judged that immediately. "That's a lie."

Of course, I knew that. "It doesn't matter," I replied, she knows where I stand with her."

Again, Miss Sally can dish it out, but she can't take it. And there comes a time when you need to look in the mirror and ask yourself if the problem is everybody else or is the problem you. After much soul searching, I told my husband I wouldn't let Miss Sally get the best of me anymore. If she chose to say and do crazy things, I was no longer wasting my time arguing with her, nor would I give her any more of my energy. I wanted to pass the test. I wanted to go to the next level. I wanted to please God, but I very well couldn't do that if I was always failing the tests that pertained to Miss Sally. And that was the beginning of the reconstruction of the pastor's wife.

How does God want us to live as pastor's wives and women in leadership? By honoring those leaders who work so hard for you, who have been given the responsibility of urging and guiding you along in your obedience. God's word is clear:

> "And now, friends, we ask you to honor those leaders who work so hard for you, who have been given the responsibility of urging and guiding you along in your obedience. Overwhelm them with appreciation and love!
>
> Get along among yourselves, each of you doing your part. Our counsel is that you warn the freeloaders to get a move on. Gently encourage the stragglers, and reach out for the exhausted, pulling them to their feet. Be patient with each person, attentive to individual needs. And be careful that when you get on each other's nerves you don't snap at each other. Look for the best in each other, and always do your best to bring it out."

1 Thessalonians 5:12-14a, 15.

Remember, the church folks are sheep, and sheep are dumb. I am not saying the people are dumb, but I am saying they have sheep-like tendencies, and we need to remember that we're sheep also. I know I give my husband a run for his money, and I also know I can be special with the church sheep as well. However, I am learning after 30 years that life is short, and time is winding up. We need to do everything in our power to please God. I want to hear Him say, "Servant well done." I don't want Him to say, "Girl, what was with you and the other sheep-goat-members? Didn't I tell you to love them and see the best in them even if they did get on your nerves?"

"Oh yeah. That is what You said, God. My bad."

Questions, Reflections & Things to Ponder

1. Are there any members in your congregation that just drive you nuts?

2. What do you do when they throw rocks and hide their hands?

3. Do you see the best in them, or do you retaliate?

4. Read Romans 12:11-21. What do you think I could've done differently if I had considered this passage? How could I have handled Miss Sally better? What do the verses say to you? Journal and see what the Holy Spirit tells you about certain members of your congregation.

5. Write down what God tells you about yourself. Share with another friend and become prayer partners concerning certain people, their issues, and your challenges with them.

PRAYER

Father God, help me to see the best in others just like you see the best in me. As you have patience with me, let me have patience with others when they get on my nerves. Thank you for loving me. Help me to love on others when they do things that hurt my feelings or those of my family. And even when they say, "But I didn't do anything," give me the strength to treat them with kindness and love. God help me not to hit back, but to discover the beauty in everyone. Don't let me get even. Lastly, help me to honor my Leader-Husband by following him and supporting his vision. Let me be an asset and not an additional ministry burden. In Jesus Name.

Chapter 12
Just Wait Until You're in My Shoes

If I'm honest, I love it when people fail. Girl, did you just say that out loud? Yes, I did. But let me clarify the statement. I love it when the Know-it-alls think pastoring is easy and attempt to do a pastor project or live a pastor moment and fall flat on their butts. Cue my laughing out loud. It's a beautiful thing to me when it happens. I relish it, and relish in it when the fall happens, because inevitably the fall *will* happen.

My husband and his side-chick (which would be me), pastor a small congregation in Southern California. We're about five highway exits from the Happiest Place on Earth – Disneyland. And when I say a small membership, I mean less than one hundred people. You know Baptist folks – it depends on what Sunday it is if they're going to show up or not. We've got the 1st and 3rd Sunday peeps, and the 2nd and 4th party people. So, our numbers fluctuate.

I'm not the co-pastor, but I am the co-pastor, if you know what I mean. My husband tells people that before he shares a concept or idea with the boardroom, he runs it by the bedroom, which would also be me, and I see you nodding saying, "I know that's right, girl".

So, because we shepherd a smaller flock, my Pastor-Man preaches, leads Wednesday night Bible study, sings, directs the praise team/choir, collects the mail, transports the gardener to and from the gardener's two residences, does the banking, counseling, weddings, and funerals, is the backup sound man, media technician, graphic designer, website developer, social media influencer, get-you-some-life-insurance-spokesperson, and he's the property management manager. Pastor-Man does everything now except the banking; that's my new department. But people still ask, "What does the pastor do all day?"

Huh? And, since the start of the pandemic, pastoring digital disciples has placed additional duties on his, no, on *our* plates. Oh, but they—other members of the congregation—can do it! And let them tell it, they can do it better than the pastor, way better. "It's a piece of cake," they say. Okay, so do it. And when they try, SPLAT! *Ahahahahahahahaha.* Gives me such joy—such great pleasure—to hear them say, "I/We apologize, Pastor."

I. LOVE. IT. *Don't judge me.*

Some of you are saying, "She's awful."

Maybe. But my feelings are my feelings, and they're real. Most times I can control them and keep them between me and Jesus, but during the months right after the 2020 pandemic hit, the Bible's words rang true, and suddenly the word became reality. "Suddenly" was Covenant City's "word" for 2020, and boy it came with a vengeance.

"I don't think, friends, that I need to deal with the question of when all this is going to happen. You know as well as I that the day of the Master's coming can't be posted on our calendars. He won't call ahead and make an appointment any more than a burglar would. About the time everybody's walking around complacently, congratulating each other—"We've sure got it made! Now we can take it easy!" ---suddenly everything will fall apart. It's going to come as suddenly and inescapably as birth pangs to a pregnant woman" 1 Thessalonians 5:1-3(MSG).

Suddenly the world shut down: businesses, schools, life, and church. Everything closed. And when that happened, church came to the house. And because church was now at the house, our entire home became church headquarters. We even had to record the services in our church studios. Yeah, girl, our living room, our family room, our bedroom, the kitchen, and the backyard became the Cyber Sanctuary backdrop. "Oh, what fun," said no one. There were technical difficulties, natural disaster occurrences, power outages, sound issues, and celebrity meltdowns. It was the best of times; it was the worst of times ever. Tony and I just fought through all the challenges that knocked us down and punched us in the face. Whoo! Many a day we were tapping the mic for sound, "Testing, testing…can you hear me?" Fighting with Facebook to let us play music and arguing with the cable company for more Wi-Fi speed. Oh, it was a hot mess! We were a hot mess. And that brings me to why I said what I said out loud. I didn't really want our church friends to fail, but it was a reality that needed to happen.

People tell us how much they love to see me and

Tony teach together on Wednesday nights. Little do they know that came about in the pandemic. Bible study used to be taught by Tony alone on Tuesday nights. But on Tuesday, March 24, 2020, that all changed. Tony was doing his usual preparations for Facebook when he noticed he couldn't get on. He tried over and over and over, but on the fourth attempt, he asked me to try to get on live. And I couldn't either.

Then he started to panic because it was after 7pm and we were late! Sisters, oh sisters! You know your pastor-husbands and time. They hate to be late. Anyway, Tony was just a fussing and cussing when I suggested we try the kids' phones. So, Tony asked Sagel II for his phone, Sydni for her phone, Jonathan for his phone, and Kennedy for her phone. None of them worked. None of the iPhones would connect to Facebook.

Now Tony was really on the ceiling because he couldn't get on Facebook to tell his adoring fans he couldn't get on. I just sat in the crushed red suede chair waiting on him to come off the ceiling. When he gets that way, I just stay quiet. That way he doesn't have an excuse to yell at me, although on that night it didn't matter anyway.

So, I keep trying to get on Facebook and finally I do! I said to him, "I'm on, I'm on," and handed him my phone. He started talking, but the live suddenly ended. Then he tried again on his phone—nothing. So, I tried again, and it comes on! By now he's aggravated, he's irritated, but he has this really strange look on his face, like he heard something or had an epiphany. He said, "Just tell everybody we'll be on tomorrow at 7 o'clock—together."

And that was it. He was eerily calm, and I repeated what he told me to say on Facebook Live, and everybody who heard the announcement said, "Cool, see you tomorrow."

When the live ended, Tony was able to log on without an issue. I was able to log back on quickly too, and all the kids iPhones were able to log back onto Facebook as well.

"Hmmm," Tony looked at me and said, "Apparently, God wants us to do the Bible study together. That's what I was hearing when I couldn't get on. He said, 'You and Laura, do it together.'"

So, our first Wednesday Bible study as a couple was born, and out of that came Sunday morning worship in the house, and Sunday morning worship back in the church building, both as a couple when we returned. The template was a huge success, and because me and Tony are me and Tony, and since we've been friends since we were in the first grade, we just did us. *Us* is our back-and-forth banter, spirited discussions, lots of laughter and eye rolls, as well as five or six "Child please." We had fun. Our thought was, *Might as well be happy and have fun since we aren't going anywhere anytime soon.*

With the success of couple-teaching, Tony decided to have the assistant pastor, the outreach pastor, and their evangelist wives do a Sunday morning panel-preaching-conversation about the George Floyd death and what the effects of racism was doing to the world. We did this on stage at the church in June 2020. It went great, and because all of us were doing work and marriage ministry on Zoom, the four of them thought, how hard could it be to teach a Wednesday night Bible study or preach a Sunday sermon live on Facebook? Hard. What people didn't realize was Tony and I had already made most of the digital boo-boos and were considered the experts. Hardly.

So, when it came time for Rob and Jackie to lead a Sunday service, they just knew they wouldn't have a backyard experience like Tony and I had, where the internet signal went out right at the opening of Tony's house-church message, and we went outside to finish the service. That was a hoot and holler, because the Wi-Fi kept going in and out, and I couldn't get up onto the high stool, I was hot, Tony was hot, we were sweating, the wind was blowing, and Tony couldn't get his words straight. Or another backyard escapade gone viral when our daughter Sydni hit the record button and there I was still trying to climb up into my seat while asking her, "Are we on Facebook? Is it live? Are we live?" and she's standing behind the iPad on the tri-pod mouthing, "Yes." Clearly, it was a disaster. But it got over 1,100 views! People love a trainwreck.

Alright, so back to Rob and Jackie. It's their turn to have service in the backyard. Everybody at that time had to go through Tony's Facebook page because, well, the cyber sanctuary was new, and we didn't know what to do. No clue. It was like the Jetsons meet the Proud Family. Anyway, Rob had a karaoke mic, not a studio mic, but *a karaoke mic*, that muffled their words, so when they spoke into it, it sounded like bwhaa, bwhaa, bwhaa—like Rob had cotton in his mouth with a paper bag over his head. And then they took turns passing the mic back and forth because they didn't have their own mics.

But it gets better—they're sitting in the gazebo in

their backyard, and a gust of wind whips past their faces and blows against the karaoke mic, which then further makes the mic sound awful, and Jackie's looking at Rob like, "*What* is *going on?*" and then Rob stops preaching and turns to Jackie and says, "What?"

Tony and I just lost it. We're looking at their faces on the TV and cracking up. It was priceless. We sat in our bed and watched them go up in flames. It was *heee*-larious. The best part? Jackie was asking me questions via text the entire time they were on Facebook Live. As Rob inched closer to the end of his sermon, she texted, "I don't know how y'all do it. It ain't as easy as it looks."

You think?

"You and pastor make it look so easy."

I turned over and read the text to Tony and he said, "Uh hmm. Now they know what it's like. Now they know what we go through. No, it's not easy. At all."

Not only did we laugh about Rob and Jackie's backyard church experience, but Mike and Maritza thought it was *heee*-larious as well. But be careful when you laugh—it comes back to bite you. Mike is our Outreach Pastor, and his wife Maritza is an evangelist. Pastor Tony wanted to make everything fair, and we needed a rest, so they got their turn at an at-home Sunday worship experience, too.

Mike and Maritza had a few opportunities to laugh at us: Rob and Jackie; Tony and Laura. I knew their time was going to be epic, and they did not disappoint. When their Sunday came, Mike couldn't get on Tony's page, which is the platform we were having to use because the Covenant City page was still a monster we were learning to conquer. Mind you, Mike tried to be ahead of the game by going on a few minutes early, no, a lot of minutes early, and he still couldn't get on. So, he called in a panic, and Tony walked him through the steps to get on his page.

Confident in pastor's instructions, Mike got off the phone, and shortly after, the Facebook Live notification made a ding, and they were LIVE!

Until they weren't.

Maritza started the service with a prayer and boy did she look like she was calling down heaven. But that's all it was—a look, because the digital disciples on the feed were ferociously commenting, "No, sound, no sound, NO SOUND," but Mike and Maritza didn't see it, so they just continued. Mike took the microphone and just started talking and talking, but then he looked down at the comments and realized, "Oh snap, nobody can hear us." He proceeded to sit directly in front of the camera and talk and not talk. Of course, he finally dialed Tony for help.

In the meantime, one of the followers typed, "Technical support needed!!!"

As the Covenant City administrator I typed, "Still can't hear you...reading your lips."

All of us online could see he was panicking, so the saints started praying and writing encouraging messages.

"We are here with you Minister Neal. Take your time. God's got this!"

Then the video froze then unfroze. Joan typed in a powerful prayer, and we all joined in while Maritza went and stood behind Mike. No, the sound never came on, and the 11 minutes of torture mercifully and abruptly ended. Praise Jesus! It was over!

Didn't I tell you earlier, folks love a trainwreck. That no-sound video got 278 views! That's God—and that's a lesson. Mike and Maritza called us after the live ended and said, "We don't know what happened. I was praying and praying and when I stopped Mike said, 'There was no sound, oh dang.'"

I hollered. Tony asked, "Well what happened?"

Mike had no idea. "T, I don't know!"

Maritza chimed in, "Now we understand what you guys meant about this being hard. It was really hard, and I felt stupid 'cause nobody could hear me, and Sister Simon, now I know. We laughed at you guys and Rob and Jackie, and look at us," she said dejectedly.

I hollered some more. When I say I laughed until I cried, believe it. Tears rolled down my cheeks as I said to them on speaker, "Uh huh, now you know how me and Pastor feel sitting up in the backyard looking all crazy. It ain't as easy as it looks, is it?"

"No, no, no," she answered.

So, I threw in, "God don't like ugly, and He ain't too crazy 'bout pretty. I bet you get that analogy now, don't you?" I said as I fell out laughing again.

"This is rich," I said, "This was good. This is what I meant when I told you just wait until y'all are in my shoes."

Maritza and Mike both said, "You right, Sis." Finally, a genuine answer.

Now you see why I said I love it when they fail. *Failing, falling, potato, pahtato, come si, come sa,* whatever your word, failing brings about a valuable lesson, and an awesome new perspective. "And now, friends, we ask you to honor those leaders who work so hard for you, who have been given the responsibility of urging and guiding you along in your obedience. Overwhelm them with appreciation and love!" 1 Thessalonians 5:12-13.

After going through their own debacle and feeling as though they failed at a church-house Sunday worship experience, both couples gained a deeper understanding, a more compassionate view, and heck of a lesson about all the work pastors do, as well as all the craziness their own pastor deals with and goes through. The six of us have grown closer together because of our pandemic pain, and latte lessons. They no longer take us for granted, and neither do we take them for granted. Rob and Jackie now have their own congregation, Mike is the technical backbone of Covenant City, and Maritza is my Ninja Prayer Warrioress; she keeps all idiots and things crazy away from me.

~

Questions, Reflections, Things to Ponder

1. What things did you discover during 2020?

   a. About yourself
   b. About your life (husband, children, family)
   c. About ministry

2. Do you ever find yourself happy the know-it-all(s) in your life fail?

3. What was your takeaway from the scenarios mentioned in this chapter?

4. Have you had any similar experiences? What happened? How was it handled? What did you learn? What did or do you regret?

5. Honestly journal your responses and see where you need to adjust. Share some of your findings with your spouse, another PW, or a friend.

6. If you feel there are no adjustments necessary, write about that. I'd like to hear about it.

PRAYER

Lord, I confess my feelings of glee about the know-it-alls in my life because you already see into and know my heart. Help me to love people like Jesus loves them. Help me to be patient and attentive with them, and see the best in everyone, even when they don't do right by me. And then, let me look in the mirror at myself. Heal my heart, help me acknowledge my shortcomings, and show me where I fall short and need to change. Make the necessary adjustments in my life, oh God. In Jesus Name.

Chapter 13
I Quit!

S on, never quit on a Monday." Pastor Carl told us this. Well, he really didn't tell me, but I was standing there, and he did look at me as he said it, so I figured he was talking to both of us.

Church was special that day, and some of the goats were acting up. Pastor Carl was not a happy camper, so he shared that wise word with us after church. Lily Valley was notorious for beating up the pastor, putting out the pastor, and not paying the pastor. Their church history was epic. Pastor Carl hadn't gotten beat up and they didn't want to put him out, but they weren't paying him. He had a wife and kids back in New York, so he and his family were living a bi-coastal life, a bi-coastal marriage, and a bi-coastal raising of the children. This was Pastor Carl's second stint; I mean second tour of duty. He'd been a Valley pastor before, left, and then returned for more. But today was one of those days he was wondering why he had come back for additional nonsense, and had to remind himself, and remind us too, that we should never quit on a Monday.

How did we get to Lily Valley? Well, let me tell you about it. In 1994, while OJ Simpson was being chased, Tony and I were headed back to California on Interstate10, feeling as if something or someone was chasing us. We were actually driving at the same time as the infamous chase. We had lived in La Place, Louisiana, for a pregnancy, which is to say, nine months, and I hated it. That season of my life couldn't end quickly enough, and Tony had received a store transfer, so we were headed home. Praise God! I was already pregnant and didn't know it, and the point of explaining the timeline is for you to understand the entire context.

Even when we were living in Van Horn, Texas—before we had moved to Louisiana—we knew that Lily Valley Church wasn't the place, couldn't be the place we were called to. The enemy had evil plans to harm us and our unborn baby, because we were involved in a horrific accident right after we said we weren't going to Lily Valley. We laughed out loud so hard that bing, bang, boom, a gust of wind blew our U-Haul across I-10 and we landed on the other side of the highway upside down, windows blown out, and Tony dangling from the rooftop because he didn't have his seatbelt on. But God! God had plans and the enemy had plans. God demolished the enemy's plans, and we ended up exactly where God wanted us to be—Lily Valley Church.

Oh, and did I tell you that we walked away from that accident with just a scratch on each of us? I had an ever-so-slight piece of glass in my foot that I pulled out myself, and Tony had a cut on his elbow. No need for stitches, a band-aid, or anything. We were able to get the car in good enough running condition that we drove it home, plexiglass and all. And this all happened on Father's Day 1994.

What the enemy meant for evil; God meant for good. Basically, God had other plans, because He demolished, destroyed, and annihilated the enemy's plans, and plopped us right down exactly at the church where we didn't want to go. Yup, planted us right at Valley as soon as we got home.

"Well, Laura, how can you be so sure," You may ask? Because the people who had the same accident we had on the day before, died, and the people who had the same accident on the day after died.

And we didn't.

I would say God demolished the devil's plans and saved our lives for a purpose. That purpose would be to show up at Valley and help Pastor Carl.

When we joined Lily Valley, there was 11 members. Tony and I made 13. When I found out I was pregnant with Kennedy, she was in utero as a member in the making. Pastor Clare was known as the mentoring pastor. He loved to take younger preachers under his wing, mentor them, and teach them the ropes of pastoring. And let me say to you right now, Valley Church (VC) was a heck of a training ground. Tony and I knew we didn't want to go back to our home churches, so when one of VC's deacons called and asked us to join them, Tony and I decided to try it. Both sets of our parents also encouraged us to see what God wanted us to do.

Pastor Clare was such a sweetheart. He mentored Tony for two years. At first, Sundays were brutal. It was so pitiful I would attend my home church and then come over to The Valley after my service ended. When

I'd get there, Pastor Clare would be up preaching and stop to tell me where to sit. He liked having one person sit on each pew, that way he could say every seat was filled.

On Sundays there'd be about 15 of us, because two new people joined after us, and with Kennedy in utero, that made 16. Whoo Hoo! Days like that I didn't know whether to laugh or cry. And I hear you now, "It's not about the number, Laura, you can have church with two or three people. It's about the heart." Ok, I get that, but it is about the number when you come from a church of 800 and your husband's home church had 600, and you're used to having a band, and music, and ushers. I would've settled for a drummer!

Ah!

Sigh.

We sat there week after week, singing dry hymns with no piano, organ, drum, or tambourine accompaniment. No nothing. We didn't make a joyful noise because we couldn't. Singing dry hymns off key was bad and listening to dry hymns off key was worse. Tony would sit in the pulpit and look out into the audience. He's look at me sitting on my very own pew and just shake his head. I would look back at him, sitting on my very own pew, sad, hungry, and pregnant, wondering how much longer this was going to last. Oh, my goodness! Some days were worse than others, and some days were more than I could take. So, I'd either stay and take one for the Gipper, or I'd leave Tony there, high, and dry.

One Sunday in particular, Pastor Carl wasn't his usual cheerful self. We found out later that he had already had several chats prior to church with some of the goat members. No, I don't mean greatest of all times members, but those ornery, animal goat-like-members who gave him a lot of grief. Reverend Clare was, and still is, an easy-going man who normally didn't get upset easily. On that Sunday, however, he appeared pretty disgruntled and aggravated if you will. The poor guy ended his sermon with an exasperated sigh, a wave of his right hand, and simply said, "Come to Jesus, I'm out!"

Just kidding, just kidding, he didn't say I'm out.

But his face said it.

At least it did to me.

Nobody joined that day, nobody came up for prayer, nobody had any announcements, nobody had any words of encouragement, or anything to say, so we just took up the collection and he ended the service. When Pastor Carl came down out of the pulpit, and went into his office, Tony and I met him inside. He plopped down into his chair and said, "Son, don't ever quit on a Monday!" Then he looked at me and said, "Daughter, don't you let him quit on a Monday." Both of us promised we would never quit on a Monday. And even today we have stuck to that creed.

Pastor Clare usually said the darkest day of the week for a pastor was a Monday. He told us after a particularly frustrating Sunday that he had to look for the silver lining on those days, and that he had to look for the best in people, otherwise he'd quit. So, he made a promise to himself that he would wait it out and let the wave of despair dissipate before he made any rash decisions. He told us to pray over it, sleep on it, and then discuss it with each other before we made any decisions we might regret.

There were many days we pondered on his words, because Valley wasn't the easiest church to pastor, and the sheep-goats weren't the easiest to get along with. "Gently encourage the stragglers, and reach out for the exhausted, pulling them to their feet. Be patient with each person, attentive to individual needs" 1 Thessalonians 5:14.

And that's what Pastor Clare did until he didn't. On several occasions after that, he would point his finger and say, "Remember what I told you." And we'd laugh.

During the two years we served under Pastor Clare, it felt like an internship. Tony preached on Sundays and taught on Wednesdays. Tony sang and recruited a choir and Tony played the drums, while I taught Sunday school. It was like he was getting us ready for something somewhere, just not there at Valley.

Because we didn't know what would happen next, Tony and I started preparing for the birth of Kennedy. The parishioners were sweet, except for one or two. They hadn't had a baby or young people (Tony and I were considered young people because we were only 28) in the church since forever, so they were happy with us. Things went really well in 1994 and 1995. In 1994, Tony and I spearheaded the Pay-the-Pastor-Some-Money Campaign, and to our delight, the congregation responded! In March 1995, Kennedy made her debut, the church grew. Tony's two former bandmates and a girlfriend became VC musicians and a choir director, and we started fellowshipping and making friends with other churches again. Things were going great! But in 1996, there was a shift.

Remember I told you Pastor Clare was and still is an easy-going man? Well, he remained that, but he started to tell us more often to never quit on a Monday. That started to worry Tony, who began to comment on it when Pastor Clare would say it.

"You don't think Pastor Clare is trying to quit, do you?"

"No, Babe, he told you he'd tell you first. Plus, he said he wouldn't quit on a Monday."

Again, times were good. In 1996, Tony had three jobs, and I had one. He was working full time for an insurance company, coaching a high school girls' basketball team part time, and was the assistant pastor to Reverend Clare. He was doing a lot.

I was working as a Claims Adjuster for Allstate. We were still doing church work, but Kennedy was a year old, and I wanted to quit Allstate and be a stay-at-home mom with her. While handling a claim for an insured, I was introduced to an Amway distributor who just happened to be the person my insured rear ended. Mr. Yutaka from Huntington Beach fell in love with my customer service skills and asked me if I would consider becoming an Amway distributor. I thought it was a sign from God, so I ran it by Tony, who thought it was a great idea, and agreed to do the business with me. He said if I worked the business and made money, I could come home.

Being a distributor worked out nicely because I had had enough of the corporate drama at Allstate. I decided to work the Amway business and sell Mary Kay. Our goal, so we thought, was for Tony to apply and hopefully, get a church. Be a pastor. But we weren't too worried because we were working the Amway business.

We quickly moved up the ranks of Amway and with some of my severance pay, took a leap of faith, and went to the Amway Convention in Portland, Oregon. We left Kennedy with my parents and told Pastor Clare our plans. He thought it was marvelous, and off we went to become millionaires. We had an awesome time in Portland, learned the tricks of the trade concerning the Amway life, and thought we'd invite everyone we knew to become distributors, including Reverend Clare. We ran into only one problem—Pastor Clare quit.

Not on a Monday, but on a Sunday while we were in Portland.

Yeah. He did that on purpose. We were nowhere around and too far away to get back to him and talk him out of it.

Oh. And he recommended young Reverend Simon to take his place.

When the members called us in Portland, Tony and I frantically tried to reach him. We couldn't get a hold of him although we tried and tried and tried. He just didn't answer his phone. Never did.

Tony and I sat in the room looking at each other.

Tony just shook his head in disbelief. "He said never quit on a Monday."

Of course, I knew. "He always said never quit on a Monday."

And then we simultaneously said, "But it's Sunday."

(Simultaneous groan.)

Tony said, "I told him to tell me when he was getting tired."

"You said, he said he would let you know when he was going to quit."

"That man quit. Today."

"While we are gone."

"He did that on purpose."

"So, we couldn't say anything or talk him out of it."

Tony was pacing and still shaking his head. "I can't believe it!"

"I can't believe *him*!"

"And then he recommended me!"

"What are you going to do?"

We talked about it all night long. We never did catch up with Pastor Clare that night. And when we got up the next morning, we still talked about how he had quit. On the way to the airport and on the plane ride all the way back home, we talked about it. We were in disbelief for several reasons. First, we hadn't had a clue. Pastor Clare had not given one clue. Secondly, he promised us we'd talk about it first before he ever did anything like hand in his resignation. Lastly, he indicated if he ever did it, it wouldn't be on a Monday. And true to his word, he didn't do it on a Monday.

He did it on a Sunday.

So, we had to wait. Until Monday.

When we landed Monday night, we got our luggage and took a taxi straight to my parents' house. They only live five minutes away, but those were the longest five minutes ever. We hadn't even gotten into the house before my parents' phone started ringing. My dad said, "Well, I guess you heard Pastor Clare resigned."

Then my mom chimed in, "Yeah, he quit today during service, and then recommended you, Tony."

The town was all abuzz. The town was abuzz because Tony and I were the home-grown products of the city. Tony and I were born and raised in Orange County, California.

Tony used the house phone to call Pastor Clare, and

he answered on the first ring. Tony immediately blurted, "Pastor Clare! What happened to never quit on a Monday?"

"Son, it wasn't a Monday," he answered, "And I'm just tired. I don't want to do it anymore. Plus, you're a young man and I think you'll do a wonderful job. It's time."

And with that, Tony became the Pastor of Lily Valley on June 8, 1996. We were both 30 years old.

Reverend Clare said he didn't heed his own advice because he'd just had enough. He was sick of the arguments, sick of all the goats, the sheep, the church folks, and their agendas. He said he just didn't have the energy to fight. And some of those issues still exist.

Romans 12:6-8 says, "If you preach, just preach God's Message, nothing else; if you help, just help, don't take over; if you teach, stick to your teaching; if you give encouraging guidance, be careful that you don't get bossy; if you're put in charge, don't manipulate; if you're called to give aid to people in distress, keep your eyes open and be quick to respond; if you work with the disadvantaged, don't let yourself get irritated with them or depressed by them. Keep a smile on your face."

Pastor Clare really tried to do all those things, but somewhere in the midst, he got weary, he got irritated, he got lonely, and he got depressed. His wife was back in New York, and the bi-coastal living and commuting had finally taken its toll. He was done, so he quit.

People have no idea how much work, effort, blood, sweat, and tears goes into pastoring. The job never ends. The calls, the complaints, the emergencies, the money problems, the housing issues, the marital concerns, and more complaints just keep coming regularly.

Pastor Clare told us never quit to encourage us, but I don't think he expected he'd succumb to the very thing he warned us about. He told us Sundays were normally the roughest day of a pastor's week. Preaching, putting out fires, counseling, praying, singing, and putting out more fires can be depressing.

Our ministry now to the younger pastors and wives' is don't quit on a Monday because you had a crazy Sunday. On Sunday and Monday take a nap and rest, take time to reflect on what happened. Think about what went well and what did not, then get a good night's sleep. When you wake up on Monday morning, things will look different.

I want family, friends, and church folks to know that Sundays are workdays. Your pastor, his wife, and their kids work on Sundays. It's the family business. They go, go, go all day Sunday, then collapse Sunday night. Mondays are a time to play catch up.

Realize that it is often a nightmare on Sundays. My leg, my back, my ankle, my calf, and my left foot hurt every Sunday. Every Sunday. No one knows more about the chaos that goes on in the PW house better than another PW. It's crazy.

And don't let the enemy throw in a fight between Pastor-Man and PW before service! Whoo! That's a mess. Here it is the pastor trying to get ready to preach and now he has to think about the heated exchange he and his wife, or he and his kids, or he and the goat-like member have had before he "goes on" as on stage, as in the pulpit, and since the Pandemic, now it's as in lights, camera, action.

Life will never be the same.

Ladies, encourage your husbands on Sundays. Pray for them before they leave the house on Sunday mornings. I find that when I pray for Tony and lay hands on him, Sunday mornings go smoother for him and for me. I'm slow anyway, so I need any help I can get. Since the twins were born in 1999, I've not made it to church on time yet. That is spiritual warfare at its best. The enemy and I fight every week, rain or shine. I pray I overcome that demon.

Remember, you both can't be crazy on the same day at the same time. One of you has to be in a good place. If your husband is in a mood on Sunday, then you can't be, and if you're feeling some type of way on Sunday, then he can't be. But this one thing I do know, and I can't stress it enough: both of you can't be crazy on the same day at the same time. That won't work. That won't ever work.

I will forever give credit to a dear friend of mine for drilling this in my soul: Don't help the devil do his job. He does just fine without you helping him. (Thanks Mrs. Meredith Sheppard.)

Lastly, never quit on a Monday. A Sunday either.

~

Questions, Reflections, Things to Ponder

1. Read, then journal about 1 Thessalonians 5:13-18. What is it saying to you?

2. Read Romans 12 then write out your takeaways.

3. Why do you think Pastor Carl quit?

4. When your husband is discouraged and wants to quit, how do you help him? Write

down some of the things you do to encourage your husband on days or seasons he feels like quitting. Maybe start a small group and share with other pastor's or minister's wives; something to encourage everyone.

PRAYER

Father God, living in the fishbowl gets hard sometimes. I often want to quit when the burdens get too heavy, and the drama of the fishbowl life threatens to overwhelm me. God help me to lean on You and trust You to direct my path. Help me to be a better encourager to my husband and my friends. Let my sisters and I who share the fishbowl life come together and live the proverb of iron sharpens iron, and may we not grow weary in well doing. In Jesus Name.

Chapter 14
So What Is It?

"Mama, this is nasty," whispered Sydni as she spit out the bar-b-que beans.

"Can't be," I said. "Miss Lisa made them."

"They don't taste like hers."

"Well, let me see what Miss Lisa says." I got up and headed to Lisa's table.

"Girl," I whispered in her ear, "Did you make these beans?"

"What are those? Them ain't my beans." Lisa said this a little louder than I expected, but she was heading over to the food table in a huff, and I couldn't stop her.

As she got closer to all the dishes on the table, she saw her pot was off to the side, kind of tucked away in a grocery bag. She stretched her arm over, lifted the lid, and screamed because her pot was empty.

"What is it?" I couldn't imagine what the problem could be.

"MY POT IS EMPTY!" she shouted.

By then, Tony had walked over and asked Lisa the

same question, "What is it?"

She said, "I brought a pot of beans, and they're not here," as she showed him the empty pot. And then her face changed. "Where's Sienna?" she asked. "She's over the food…"

And just like that, Sienna appeared at Lisa's arm, smiling, "Yes? What's wrong?"

"What happened to my beans?" Lisa was questioning as she pointed to the evidence of the empty pot.

Sienna replied, "Oh I mixed them in with mine."

Lisa shrieked, "You did what? You mixed *my beans* with *your beans*? What would make you do that?"

Sienna paused and opened her mouth, but nothing came out.

Lisa turned bright red, marched back to her table, gathered up her things, stomped all the way back to her car, and left. She never came back to the picnic.

She was mad.

Sienna didn't see anything wrong with what she had done. She never did. This wasn't her first church food faux pas. She offered the pastor some beans to put on his plate, like nothing happened, but he declined, looked at me and said, "Girl, we have a problem."

And so, we stood there looking like two deer caught in the headlights. We wondered what in the world made Sienna mix her beans with Lisa's. Now we were stuck standing, glancing around while everybody watched to see if we were going to eat the blended bar-b-que beans.

Once again, we were left holding the bag.

Insert wide eyes

This is an issue we are still working on. We still don't know why Sienna Member mixed the beans, and why she mixed the beans without asking. It could've been a number of things, but we never found out. Why do you think Sienna mixed the beans together?

_____
_____
_____
_____
_____.

~

"We cleaned out our trailer, getting ready for our move, and I came across this and wanted you have it," said Carla Member as she handed the heavy picnic basket to me. The very old picnic basket was heavy because it contained silverware—lots of silverware with hard plastic-colored handles: red and yellow ones, silver metal ones, and disposable white plastic forks, spoons, and knives. Oh, and those old-school thin paper plates with the scalloped edges that looked and felt as if they were 20 years old. The items were all encased in separate Zip Loc bags. with a ton of napkins—not the pretty kind, but the generic white and brown kind you got from restaurants all smashed together like they too were 20 years old. *Think what is this?*

"Oh, how nice," I said, not wanting to hurt her feelings, but knowing full well I had no use for the picnic basket. "Thank you for thinking of us," my voice trailing off as I walked out the church to my car. But as soon as I got to my car and unlocked the door, Carla Member had followed me outside and was standing right behind me reaching for the basket as I tried to put it in the backseat.

"Wait, let me show you what's inside the basket," she insisted. So, I turned around and held up the basket as she rummaged through to show me all the stuff I— we (me, pastor, and the kids) were getting. *Great,* I thought. *More junk to clutter up my house while she cleared out said junk from her house.*

Yay me.

We used to be the dumping ground for all the church extras when Tony first became the pastor. We were a young family that didn't have a lot, so the members felt it was their duty to fill up our new house with stuff. Some of the extra stuff was new, and some of it was not. We got "blessed" with extra food, extra clothes that didn't even look like us or fit us, extra books, extra paintings, extra blankets, extra soda machines—like the home and vending kind, and just extra, extra, extra anything and everything. Now I think it's become a habit that they don't know how or even want to break.

Stop giving junk under the guise of helping or giving. If the person doesn't need it, don't offer it. Like the time it was the Pastor and Wife's Appreciation Month and Sister Lily Weak wanted the pastor's wife to have a fur stole. She gave me her 1972 fox-mink-rabbit fur stole and pulled it out of a Hefty Kitchen trash bag.

Wide eyes

Or the time when Alli Member brought my favorite dish to church so I wouldn't have to cook dinner on Sunday, but my favorite dish was collard greens and Alli brought me a ginormous pot of not-so-seasoned-well-turnip greens.

Yeah, we're not going to eat that.

Oh, and then there was Marsha Member who had a

dog that lived in her the house and ate in her kitchen while she prepared food. But Marsha Member always wanted to be the head chef responsible for cooking everything on special church days, especially when the church expected a lot of people.

I see you thinking. *A dog in the kitchen while you cook?*

Exactly.

No ma'am.

No sir.

Uhhhh, that would be a no.

And let's just stop right here and address the elephant in the room. It has to be said. Consider this a hard conversation moment. Black people do not allow their pets in the kitchen while they cook. If you prepare your food with your canine companion beside you, they/we will not eat the food you cooked or prepared at your house with your pet. Especially if it's a dog, and most definitely not if it's a cat. Like most people, I think, we hate any type of hair in our food; pet hair, human hair, whatever kind of hair, in our food – accidental or not. The abovementioned is a very important rule. Please remember it. Put it in your mind's rolodex. If you want to discuss it with me later, text me and we'll chat.

And I've saved the best for last. I just love the parishioners who sabotage my weight loss efforts. You may want to give them the benefit of the doubt and contend that they mean well, but they don't. And I know it. If the pastor's wife says she's watching calories, or making lifestyle changes for the family, especially for the pastor, or if she says she's dieting, that's code for, "Don't bake, bring, or buy any desserts, sodas, or super rich foods for her or the family. It'll be in the trash somewhere. Don't waste your time and hard effort." However, sometimes the PW won't throw it all away. She might freeze some and throw away the rest; that way she's honest when she says, "It was delicious, but I only ate a little bit."

Okay. That wasn't the truth. That was a lie. We don't eat any of it.

Shhhh, with index finger touching lips, don't tell them I told you.

"Get along among yourselves, each of you doing your part...Be patient with each person, attentive to individual needs. And be careful that when you get on each other's nerves you don't snap at each other. Look for the best in each other, and always do your best to bring it out" 1 Thessalonians 5:13-15.

Here's the thing, I want to be totally transparent when I say this, as in super sincere, if there is such a thing. Paul writes about the way God wants us to live; how we should honor leaders, treat people in authority, encourage stragglers, help the tired, and be patient with everyone. Friends, I want to please God and hear Him say well done. I know we all want to do better when it comes to the church members, even if they do give us grief, share their junk, and sabotage our healthy living efforts. God wants us to run the race with patience, remain focused, and stay in our lane as we help build His kingdom. Let's do our best, and God will take care of the rest.

~

Questions, Reflections, Things to Ponder

1. Have you had any issues with your culinary ministry? How have you handled your family and church feeding challenges, if any?

2. Do your members give you unwanted items or do they purchase you and your husband and family new items?

3. Does your family eat foods from all church members/families? Why or why not?

4. What do you tell your congregation about your food preferences?

5. Read and reflect on 1 Thessalonians 5. Write down any aha moments or takeaways. Find and discuss your thoughts about this chapter with another PW. Are any of your situations the same, similar, or different?

PRAYER

Lord, I know we are all different. Help me to be more patient with others, show more compassion to others, more grace, more mercy, and forgive those who do opposite of the vision. God, help me to see the best in everyone, and to lean on You instead of my own understanding. Father God, I so want to please You. Help me to be the woman You have called me to be. In Jesus Name.

Chapter 15
Please Stop: The Pastor *Can* Do Wrong

There's this myth going around that the pastor can do no wrong. If you're a PW, you know exactly what I'm talking about. And if you're not a PW, you're going to find out.

The Sisterhood is tight, and I'll probably get in trouble for sharing some of the Pastor-Man's shenanigans, but look, folks need to know that their pastor can do wrong.

"Oh, Sister Simon you're so hard on the pastor." He didn't do anything wrong," says Roberta Church Member.

"You're always getting on him."

"You are so mean to Pastor."

"Why you be looking at the pastor that way?"

"Stop mad-dogging the Pastor."

"You always coming in church like you want to punch the pastor."

These are just some of the statements I hear about the man of God some folks call their pastor. Now don't get me wrong, my guy is a good dude, but he has his moments. I might get in trouble with what I say out loud, but, hey, confession's good for the soul, right?

If you let the church members tell it, there's a picture of my husband right next to the dictionary definition of sainthood. Ha! I'm here to dispel the myth that PWs are unnecessarily hard on the pastor-man for no reason; no good reason at all. Y'all don't know that the wonderful guy you see as Pastor-Man on Sundays can be Atilla the Hun or Psycho Bob (as Jackie Harris calls her Pastor-Man) Monday through Saturday.

People laugh when I tell them Pastor doesn't like to share. They can't believe it. Not "they" pastor.

"Oh no, he's not like that."

"You're making that up, First Lady."

I simply say, come on by. Stay awhile, then talk to me later.

As a young couple who pastored folks who were more like family than church members. we opened our house to anyone who needed a place to stay until they got on their feet. We had Gail, Terence and Jeannie, Mike and Maritza, Shameika, Aisha, Roberta, Missi, and Anyea. And they don't mind me sharing their Simon Stories because they've already shared them publicly.

Gail was my college sorority sister who stayed with us just a short while until she married Tony's friend, Robert.

Terence and Jeannie stayed with us until escrow closed on their house.

Mike and Maritza and their kids stayed until their new place was ready.

Shameika and Aisha were working and going to college, so they stayed with us during their off and on time.

Roberta stayed the longest—two years.

Missi moved from Spain and stayed awhile, and Anyea stayed a minute.

Here's the thing: everybody was either a friend or relative, so they knew the real Tony Simon. But Miss Roberta was a church family member who wore the rose-colored glasses. She thought her pastor could do no wrong and was one of the main ones who gave me the most grief about "her pastor." When she came to live with us, the scales fell off her eyes, and I loved it.

I was a transparent PW who didn't mind sharing because it was so much easier than lying. Roberta was an older woman whose boyfriend was a preacher, so she knew the drill, or so she thought. One night Tony and I had an epic argument. He didn't care who was in the house, and he wasn't backing down. And he didn't back down. We both yelled and screamed and yelled and screamed and cussed and shouted and then I stopped and went downstairs to sit in the living room in the dark. Phew! Since Roberta and the kids heard all the commotion, she came downstairs to sit with me and talk. She really thought I needed some company after hearing all the things Pastor Man had said.

When she sat down in the wing chair next to me, I started laughing. She looked at me and asked, "Are you okay?"

I stopped laughing long enough to respond, "Yes, I'm good. Did you hear your guy?"

She smiled, "Yes, we heard him. Everybody heard him." And then we both laughed.

I guess Tony Simon heard us and thought we were having too much fun, so down the stairs he came and caught us laughing.

"What's so funny?" he asked.

"You," I laughed.

"Oh really," he said while snatching my book I was reading out of my hand.

"Yes, really," I said, and he proceeded to rip my hard cover book almost in half! Although he did struggle a bit, I was impressed! He actually tore the book! And then he handed it back to me. Ooo-wee! Talk about eyes wide open; hers were. I handed the book to Roberta as he ran back up the stairs.

I leaned over to Roberta and whispered, "So what you think about your pastor now?" Then I sat back and started laughing again. "Ah huh, now you see what I've been telling you. He's a piece of work and none of y'all believe me."

Her eyes were still popping out of her head. "Girl, he ripped that hard cover book in half! He sho' nuff was mad."

I agreed and told her this is all I wanted her to see—the other side.

The Pandemic 2020 was a stressful time for pastors and their families because we hadn't ever had to do everything ourselves. When the staff got the chance to come back and have live church in the middle of 2020, we were excited. That meant we had some help again. One particular Saturday, we combined praise team rehearsal with media ministry so we could kill two birds with one stone: the stone being planning for cyber church the next day. Y'all remember that Pandemic Moment?

Pastor Man was irritated and aggravated because the sound wasn't sounding right. He was in one of his rude moods, and we all knew it. Tony was going back and forth, walking up to the stage and back to the sound booth, and he did it about 18 times. He acted like he didn't want our (Maritza, Gwen, and Laura) help, so we sat on the stage and laughed and joked. Then Rude Boy came up and asked, "How does it sound?"

"What sound?" Maritza asked.

"What sound?" Gwen asked.

"What sound?" I asked.

And he went off—not on them, but on me! Mike was standing behind him when Tony decided to be The Grinch, and Mike had this look on his face like, "No pastor did not just act crazy with Sister Simon just now." Gwen and Maritza looked at each other with the same look Mike had, and then I looked at everybody, including Mike who was still standing behind Pastor Man who didn't know it. My expression said, "See, see? I told you so."

Tony Simon was in rare form that day, and was short and snappy and cranky, so I said, "You didn't have to say it like that, and you didn't have to be ugly to me. We didn't know what you were talking about. You didn't say the type of sound you were looking for."

He snapped back, "I was not, and I did not."

Okay.

As Tony turned around and walked back to the sound booth again, Mike, Maritza, and Gwen said, "That wasn't cool. That was not okay how he talked to you."

So, I said, "Then y'all tell him. He won't hear it from me."

The crew let him be his persnickety self, and I went home so I wouldn't say anything crazy and disrespectful. The Lord has beat me enough regarding

Tony Simon. Two wrongs don't make a right, so I left while I could. Mike and Maritza called me and said, "We're going to talk to pastor because that wasn't right."

My only response was, "Okay."

Later that afternoon when he got home, Pastor Man and I talked. It was a great talk and he asked me what was it that he said that made me so upset. I explained to him what happened. How he was rude and crotchety. Mike had been standing right behind him the entire time and didn't like his words nor his tone.

He had calmed down by then and apologized but didn't want to hear what Mike and Maritza had to say, which said to me he was just blowing smoke to appease me. I let him apologize again, but I told him as pastor, he had to be mindful of his members. They hadn't seen him in fool mode in a long time. I reminded him that they lived with us years ago, and they'd forgotten about his temper. Lastly, I said, "You need to apologize to them."

"For what?" he asked.

"For being rude and nasty."

"Well, I didn't say it any type of way."

"But you did, and I wouldn't say anything, or you wouldn't feel bad or apologize if you hadn't said it any type of way. You know how you sounded."

But okay, you don't have to worry about me, you don't have to worry about me! In my Tik Tok version voice.

True to their word, Mike and Maritza came over instead of calling. And when they got to the house, we all sat in the living room as Mike and Maritza proceeded to tell their pastor he was out of order with his words, his tone, and his actions. Whoo! God vindicated me quick, fast, and in a hurry! It didn't take long at all. "Vengeance *is* Mine, I will repay," says the Lord" Romans 12:19 NKJV.

Baby, it took less than two hours for the Lord my God to avenge me. "Do not be overcome by evil, but overcome evil with good" Romans 12:21 NKJV. I was so glad I passed the test. It felt so good to let the Lord fight my battle. In my spirit, God had said, "Girl, you don't have to worry about him, I'll handle it." And just like that, no argument, no ugly words, just me and Jesus handling Brother Tony. In the olden days, when I was younger, I wanted to make sure Tony heard me, so I'd fight until I got my point across. He wasn't going to have the last word. But this was not my fight. "Don't insist on getting even; that's not for you to do. I'll do the judging," says God. "I'll take care of it." Romans 12:17-19. When you turn it over to God, He'll handle it, and you won't even have to get your hands dirty.

Sister, and I am being sincere, I know you want to scream sometimes with aggravation when Pastor-Husband does you dirty. But don't you worry about it. In due season, in God's time, He will make it right. He will work it out for you. And He will make everything work out for good. Remember, your husband is God's Man, and God will work *His* Man out!

Don't give up.

"Don't quit in hard times; pray all the harder. Help needy Christians be inventive in hospitality," Romans 12:13. And when it gets hard, because it will, pray even more. God will answer you if you will just be obedient to Him and His word. The pastor can do wrong because he's human. There is a way to show the parishioners your guy can be just like them at times. We all fall short, and that includes the pastor.

And we'd all do well to remember that.

Questions, Reflections, Things to Ponder

1. Does your Pastor Man ever get out of hand?
2. When or if he does, how do you handle it?
3. Do you go to God first or later?
4. What do you when the church folks think the pastor does no wrong? Do you tell them differently or let God remove the covers from their eyes?
5. Journal your thoughts about this chapter. How would you have handled the situation? Has this happened with any of your church members and the pastor? Read Romans 12:13-19 and write down your thoughts after meditating on the verses.

~

Suggestion from Laura: Tony has figured out that if I don't argue with him, there is no argument. In the sixth year of our marriage, I learned to stop yelling and going tit-for-tat with Tony and just start praying. Yup. When we argue and he won't stop although I have, I bust into a prayer. I pray for him, I pray for me, I pray for us, and watch God God-handle him. Or me, if necessary. Sometimes it's me, and the Holy Spirit will turn the tables on *me*. This strategy never fails. Remember, he belongs to God.

The Man of God is totally knocked off guard when you stop fighting and turn the reins over to the Lord. God can get your guy back in line quicker than you ever can. I promise. Try it, not as manipulation, but as seeking sincere help from the Lord. He wants to help you. Take Him up on His offer.

~

PRAYER

Lord, I'm not always in the mood or frame of mind to hear from You when it comes to having those difficult discussions with my man. Help me to remember there is never any justification for harsh words. Lord, lead me and guide me in the way I should speak to my husband after a heated discussion. Tell me what to say and if I should even say anything at all. God, I want to be more Christlike in all areas of my marriage and relationships. Let my speech be edifying and uplifting to my brothers and sisters in Christ, and let my words be a testimony of Your grace to my sisters and brothers. Lord continue to remind me that I am Your child and to act like it. In Jesus Name.

Chapter 16
She Said I Murdered My Children

In 1997 I had my first ectopic pregnancy. Kennedy was two years old, and I was a fourth-grade teacher. I was nine weeks pregnant, and I had told my doctor I thought it might be an ectopic pregnancy because I was spotting, and I just didn't feel right. Looking back on it, I didn't even feel pregnant, but Tony chocked it up to me reading about all these symptoms on the internet. At that time, the Macs were in all the classrooms at my school, so I would stay after work daily and look stuff up. In my gut, I knew it was an ectopic pregnancy, but my doctor, who was a female, said, "Eh, just wait until your next visit, you'll be about 12 weeks and we can take a look then. Spotting is normal. You'll be fine." Now that statement was after my third phone call. Nobody believed me.

One of the older teachers had had an ectopic pregnancy, and she said, "Maybe you should see another doctor, you know, get a second opinion. I think you know your own body, and you've been pregnant before. I'd call again and make them see you."

And so, I tried calling again to make an appointment or at least to get a referral to see another doctor as soon as possible. I called from my classroom and scheduled an appointment two weeks out, but I started feeling sick and a little dizzy at school and thought, "She's nuts. Something's wrong with me." But for whatever reason, although I see the hand of God all over the situation now, I didn't leave that day until I felt my classroom décor was complete, and my lesson plans were ready for the week. I finished up, walked down the many stairs to my car, and headed to the babysitter's house to pick up Kennedy.

The babysitter was only a few blocks away from the school where I was teaching, and the babysitter was Libni's mother, one of my students. On most days, Libni would stay after school with me, and then I'd take her home when I picked up Kennedy, so she was in the car with me.

As we pulled up to her house, I felt an awful twinge on my right side and doubled over in pain. I told Libni to run to the house, and when I could, I would walk there. After sitting in the car for what seemed like an eternity, I was able to pull myself up and roll out of the car. I slowly made it to the house and Libni's mom said in Spanish, "Mrs. Simon, you don't look so good."

I told Libni to tell her mom I didn't feel well and to ask if I could just sit down for a minute. We all went into the living room, and I sat on the floor because there was no furniture in the front room. I started sweating profusely and feeling nauseous, so I got up and stumbled to the bathroom. I barely made it to the toilet before everything started pouring out of my mouth and my butt, and my stomach was growing larger by the second. Ohhhhh, things were bad!

I called out to Libni to call my husband and tell him I'm sick and could he pick me up and take me to the hospital. They didn't have a house phone nor a cell phone, so Libni had to go across the street to the lawyer's office and ask them to use their phone. When she came back, she told me my husband was on his way. After everything stopped pouring out of my body, and after I could get myself cleaned up, I laid down on the tile floor with my face pressed against it to cool my body off; I was burning up! I laid there until Tony came and put me in our truck with Kennedy. He took one look at me and told me to call the doctor and see what she recommended. So, I called her office and put her on speaker—she told Tony to get me to the emergency room—fast! Thank God UCI Medical Center was only two blocks away from our house. Tony got me there in 10 seconds. *Insert wide eyes*

Tony ran in and told them I needed a wheelchair because I was too weak to walk. The admitting clerk rushed out to get me, but while she wheeled me in, she asked me a gazillion questions. I remember I could barely respond to her. After the third no response she finally looked at me, like really *looked* at me and said, "Let me get a nurse to take your blood pressure 'cause you don't look so good." Then she leaned in closer from across the table and continued, "You actually look green." She waved to the nurse behind her and said, "Come take her blood pressure; she doesn't look so good."

The other nurse scurried over and put the cuff on my arm because by then, my chin was on my chest, my head was in my lap, and my stomach was steadily puffing up. The poor nurse was pumping and stopping the blood pressure cup, pumping and stopping until she finally got a reading of 30/60 or something with a 30 and a 60 and she started to panic-scream. She wheeled me around and yelled, "Get her back there, get her back there, move, move! She has no blood pressure!" Then she leaned down to me and said, "You have no blood pressure." Then to nobody in particular but to everybody in the room, she hollered, "She's bleeding somewhere!" And finally, back to the back we went.

Believe it or not, it got worse. They knew I was bleeding internally; told me I probably lost the baby, (insert you are stupid look), *I already knew that*, and we need to do a transvaginal ultrasound to confirm what we think happened. Meanwhile I'm on the table asking Tony, "Do you think I'm going to die like this? But wait, take Kennedy to Miss Toni and Kristy so she doesn't see me like this, doesn't remember me like this…" I trailed off.

"No, you're not going to die like this." Tony tried to comfort me. "And I'll take Kennedy after they tell me what's going on."

I laid there and cried because I told that dumb doctor my pregnancy was ectopic! I felt like something exploded inside of me—and I was right. My right fallopian tube had ruptured, and I was in critical condition. But wait, I hadn't had the ultrasound yet.

All I remember is being wheeled to the back part of the hospital for the ultrasound by a sweet young man. He was nervous because there wasn't a female technician on duty, and he was the only one who could take care of me. He would be doing the ultrasound procedure by himself. I was thinking, *Man, I don't care, just get it done*, but I felt like I had to use the bathroom, so I asked him to help me up and get me to the bathroom. He helped me to the bathroom, and as he closed the door, he said, "If you need anything, just call out and I'll get someone to help you." That was code for, if you need help let me know so I can get a woman to come get you. (*Cue the soap opera music.*)

I sat on the toilet forever, but nothing came out. And since nothing came out, I tried to get up. But I was dizzy, my legs were wobbly, and I went down. I fell at the base of the toilet but in the crevice over by the sink. I was laying in an awkward position and couldn't lift myself up. So, I stayed there for a while and prayed and asked God to please not let me die here alone in this bathroom. I begged Him to send someone without me having to holler out. Yeah. Then I thought, *I don't want to call out to this guy, he's going to $\$*^\#$ on himself.* At that moment, the young man said, "Mrs. Simon, are you ok? Do you need help?"

Without hesitation I shouted, "Yes, I need help so come on in!"

"Let me go get a female," he said, and I screamed back, "No. You open the door and come help me! I don't care if you're a man!"

He quickly opened the door and saw me sprawled out on the tile with my gown bunched up to my stomach, exposing all my lady parts, and his face drained of every ounce of color. He looked away because he was embarrassed and he thought I was too, so I helped him out and said, "Come on here. Bend down and help me up." and I quickly added, "and no, I will not sue you for sexual harassment because you saw my vagina. You're already gonna do my ultrasound."

But to his relief, after he helped me up, a female technician came in and said she was going to do the procedure instead of him. He almost fainted, but finally gave me a smile.

I got myself on the table and Marcy explained the procedure. All I could think was, "Let's do this already. I know the baby is gone."

Marcy proceeded to insert the wand into my vagina and said, "We must do surgery, there is no baby. I'm sorry Miss Simon."

I looked back at her and said, "I already knew there was no baby, so let's just get it over with."

She finished up and wheeled me back to my emergency room spot where I met Tony, Kennedy, more nurses, and the anesthesiologist. While one nurse was putting the surgery cap on my head, everybody was talking at the same time about what was going to happen next. I told everyone I was good and to let my husband pray for me before they wheeled me back. Tony prayed, let me kiss Kennedy, then he kissed me, and he was about to leave when I whispered, "Uhm, if I'm having surgery, don't I need to take my contacts out?" Everyone started hustling and bustling trying to find containers and saline solution for my contacts saying, "Oh Lord, yes, you need to get them out of your eyes!" They got it done and wheeled me back.

When I woke up, I was covered in warm blankets but shivering uncontrollably. The nurse came over to me and said everything went well and they'd be taking me to my own private room now that I was awake. Then the doctor, who was a female teaching resident, came over to explain that although the surgery went well, I would be weak for a while and out of commission at least eight weeks. I was not to walk up and down any stairs, I was only to use elevators, I needed bedrest, and I was to do no heavy lifting. It turned out I was right—I had had an ectopic pregnancy, and yes, my right fallopian tube had ruptured, and they had to remove it. But not to worry, I'd still be able to have more children.

Why couldn't my doctor just have listened to me? Then this never would've happened. And then the tears started to fall.

Here's the interactive part of the book. Now you tell me, what part of the story made me sound like a woman who murdered her child?

I'll wait.

_____

_____

_____

Let's move forward to 2001, four years since the emergency surgery, and I get a card in the mail from a former member who had moved to the East coast. Now mind you, the first ectopic was in 1997, the twins were born in 1999, and the second ectopic was two years later. That 2001 pregnancy was ectopic, and it also resulted in surgery, but it was caught in time, so I didn't lose another fallopian tube, but lots of drama and trauma transpired with that pregnancy also.

So, I'm going to ask you again—with all that my body went through between 1997 and 2001, did I come off to you as a woman who would murder her children?

Take a sip.

Let me be clear, I most assuredly love God, and I know vengeance is His, and it's 2022, but I still feel some type of way about the woman who sent me that crazy "encouragement card" back in 2001. I'd had three pregnancies and three surgeries, with the third one being in 2001, the same year Andrea Yates had her meltdown, and you have the audacity to write in a card, "We don't want another Andrea Yates on our hands." And that did it. That right there sent me over the ledge—not edge, as in a fall, but the ledge, as in a jump to fall on a sword.

What makes people think they can just say anything? Deliver me from the holy old lady who thinks she can say anything she wants to you under the guise of concern. Girl, pahleez, I'm 'bout sick of that life. And as PWs, we are expected to just take it, like we don't have one nerve for them to get on. Sigh. I digress, let me finish this.

The Women of Wisdom, affectionately known as WOW did one of my first Bible and book studies together in 2001. I was a lover of Mike Murdock and his book *The Assignment.* I chose the book for its phenomenal principles and simplistic, yet powerful chapters. The ladies and I enjoyed the narrative and had lots of material for spirited discussions.

One Thursday night, I came to the women's study rather heated. Earlier that day I had received a card in the mail from the former senior member who moved to the East coast. She was one of those holy know-it-alls who left to take care of a sick family member, and later stayed there so she could purchase a house. At that time, the housing market was fantastic in the Southeast.

Anyway, while she attended our church, she was the type of member who told us how to pray, when to pray, what to look for when Jesus came back, the 5000 names of Christ, when to take communion but don't call it communion, when to take what sacraments, and what each sacrament meant, what bread to eat, what bread not to eat, when to drink holy water, what time to drink the holy water, where to sprinkle it or not sprinkle it, what was considered pagan, why we shouldn't celebrate the holidays, and oh my stars, the list goes on and on and on. Let's just say when she left, I missed her, but I didn't.

So, I remember it being a summer meeting because it was still light outside, and I couldn't wait for the ladies to get to the church. We held the class in the social hall, since the men were in the sanctuary, and I pulled out the card and laid it on the table.

Andrea Yates was the hot topic that summer. She was the mother of five children from Houston, Texas, who murdered all five of her children June 20, 2001. She had four sons and one daughter ranging in age from seven years to six months. I remember the details of the brutal crime because the twins were 18 months old, Kennedy was six years old, and I had become a stay-at-home mom. The story hit me especially hard because the twins were walking and talking and getting into everything. Keeping up with them was a full-time job.

I understood postpartum depression very well and felt sorry for Andrea Yates. I knew the June 20th date because it was the wedding anniversary of a good friend. We had a conversation on that date about postpartum depression and the state of new mothers' mental health. The story transfixed the nation and transfixed me. I just couldn't believe a woman could chase down her five babies, submerge them under bath water, and drown every one of them. I mean, yeah, I was depressed, but that seemed a little extreme, and I'd been praying for her since I heard the tragic news. But imagine my horror when I received a card that compared me to Andrea Yates!

Are you kidding me?

To add insult to injury, I was excited to get the card. It arrived in a bright yellow envelope, and I saw it was from Mary Chandler. I quickly opened it although I was a little wary about what it contained. I opened the envelope and pulled out a lovely pastel card with a gorgeous flower arrangement on the front. *Ah, Miss Mary did all right, I thought to myself.* And then I opened the card and began to read:

Dear Sister Simon,

> Hope all is well and you and pastor and the kids are doing well. I heard the church is doing well and growing. They told me about your recent pregnancy, and I know you, but you need to take care of yourself and think about if you should have any more babies or not, because we don't want another Andrea Yates on our hands, do we? Get your rest and take care of yourself. Yahweh is good. God Bless you in the name of Yeshua,

Miss Mary Chandler

I lost it. Literally. I remember being in the living room just screaming at the top of my lungs. I said a whole lot of not nice words. Loudly. Let me tell you, Jesus was not pleased with me, but my reasoning to God was, *She's got a lot of nerve!* I read the card over and over and over again. Each time I got madder and madder. I was flamin' hot! Had she lost her mind? I had two, not one, but two ectopic pregnancies and she compared me to a woman who had run her children down, dragged them back to the house, held them under water, and drowned them. I was beyond livid.

I got so hyped as I shared the card with the ladies that they became enraged as well. That evening was not a good look for any of us. Eventually we calmed down and I decided to make this situation a teachable moment. We were already studying *The Assignment*, which I highly recommend by the way, and as a group we decided to let me write her a letter, and they would send her cards based on the writings of Mike Murdock. We would make this a real-life application. I went home and wrote a 13-page letter, and each lady picked her own card, wrote something just as crazy as Miss Chandler did, sealed it up all nice and pretty, and they brought their cards back to me the following week.

Petty me collected the cards, put them in a large brown envelope along with my 13-page letter, and mailed the package to Sister Miss Can't-Believe-You-Sent-Me-A-Card-Comparing-Me-To-Andrea-Yates.
When she received the package, read the letter and all the cards, she called my husband to say she was hurt by my actions. She didn't bother apologizing to me, but thought she was doing something by telling the pastor.

Not.

She wasn't that hurt. Couldn't have been. She didn't call me. But when she did get the nerve to talk to me, I told her in no uncertain terms that I wasn't sorry I wrote or sent the letter. I told her she must've been out of her mind for comparing me to Andrea Yates.

I said, "Essentially, you said I murdered the two ectopic babies, and I was crazy like Andrea Yates. I was and still am offended. I'm even more aggravated that you would tell my husband and not come to me.

You were big and bad enough to call me Andrea Yates, so be big and bad enough to tell me you think I'm crazy. And you act as if I killed my babies—like I had control over my ruptured fallopian tube. Like I had control over my baby growing in the wrong spot!"

She upset me so. I was angry. I was disappointed. I was hurt. Even now the memory just makes me sad. The fact that she compared my miscarriages to murder still blows me away. What was she thinking? What made her come to that conclusion? When I see a 57-year-old Andrea Yates, who waives her annual get out of jail rights to remain in the mental hospital she's been in since 2001, I feel for her, and it takes me back to 2001 every time. Sister Miss Mary Chandler really called me Andrea Yates.

But wait, it gets better. A few years ago, after my twins graduated from high school, and 14 years after the Andrea Yates card situation, Miss Mary's son runs into my husband at the school and told him he wanted to talk. He had been a member of our church also at the same time his mother was. Although she moved, he and his family had continued to attend our church. But, after a while, they moved, and left our church. In 2018, the son finally told my husband the real reason they left the church: it over the 2001 shenanigans with his mother.

So, here's how PWs get a bad rap. Miss Mary's son told Tony that he thought I was too hard on his mom about the crazy card. He said he thought I took it the wrong way, and his mother was simply trying to help.

Are you serious? *Laugh out loud. Pause.* Tony took up for me, though. I was a proud wife. "Your mother was wrong, Spencer, and my wife just made it a teachable moment. I hate that you couldn't tell me this years ago. We could've talked about it and hopefully reconciled like my wife and your mother."

That is the reason living life in the fishbowl is not for the faint of heart.

But God is good, and God is faithful. He reminded me of the go-to verse I've had since 2001, "If it is possible, as much as depends on you, live peaceably with all men" Romans 12:18 (NKJV). During the 2020 Pandemic, I discovered the Message version which says, "Don't hit back; discover beauty in everyone. If you've got it in you, get along with everybody. Don't insist on getting even; that's not for you to do, 'I'll do the judging,' says God. 'I'll take care of it'" Romans 12:17-19.

Has someone offended you? Have they said something totally crazy or inappropriate that has or had you on the ledge? Or the edge? It's okay, it's okay. God will take care of it. I promise.

~

Questions, Reflections, Things to Ponder

Have you ever had a situation like this?

1. What did you do?
2. How did you feel?
3. What did God do about it?
4. Read and reflect on Romans 12:14-19. Journal your takeaways and conversations with God.
5. Email your takeaways to me. I'd love to hear them. laurasimonauthor@gmail.com

PRAYER

Lord, You know my heart, what I've been through,

what hurtful things people have said and done. Help me to come to You and let you avenge me. Don't let my injured pride get in the way of healing and reconciliation. Touch my heart. Let me bless my frenemies and no cussing them out. Help me not to hit back. Help me discover the beauty and see the best in everyone. No more getting even; that's for You to do. I love You and thank You in Jesus Name.

Chapter 17
You Want Me to Do *Whaaaaaat?*

Forgiveness isn't for you; it's for the other person. The other person may never apologize.

You might not ever get an apology.

Forgiveness will make you feel better.

If you forgive, God will forgive you.

You've heard all those statements before, haven't you? I mean, I know you've seen the list of truths people want to tell you about forgiveness. Well, what if I don't want to forgive?

It's not fair.

It wasn't even my fault.

I didn't do anything wrong, so why am I the one who has to forgive?

I don't mean to yell. Really, I don't. It's just that I do well for a while, and then a trigger hits. Some days I can manage the triggers, go to God, and just bask in His love and attention. Other days I'm mad as hell and just don't get why I have to go through this. I know forgiveness is a process. I know what the Bible says. I get all that. But some days I'm just like, "*Whatever.*"

Do you have days like that? Mine just happens to be with PastorMan, my husband. For you, it may be someone or something else. But for me . . .

First, don't judge me. What you're about to hear is the real, raw, and honest truth—my truth. Pray for me as you read it. Pray for yourself if it makes you feel some type of way. Pray for the sisters you know who might be in denial and don't want to face it. Betrayal is betrayal. Any kind. Period. My kind though, is the husband kind.

In our 19th year of marriage, the husband decided he was going to have an affair. It started out emotionally and eventually became a full-fledged physical affair. You know, the kind you divorce a person over. As you're reading this, let me tell you that it took a lot out of me to write this down on paper. And I'm telling you this because I really want to set someone free. Who it is, I may never know, but I want you to know you are not alone on your journey, and you're not alone in feeling the way you feel.

I love God. I trust God. But some days I'm mad at God. Yep. I said that out loud. It is not easy for me to say that, but it is necessary for you to know. Maybe you're in a place like me. I love my marriage now, but I am so pissed off that I had to go this route to get it. This right here (this feeling) is not a pleasant one.

So, back to my story.

Never say never, and don't forget that some words will always come back to haunt you. Remember that.

I'm an only child, so growing up I was always in the company of adults. I heard too much, and I saw too much, which meant I knew too much. I was adulting at the age of eight. I can hear you asking, "Girl, how did you come to know so much at such a young age?"

Well, my father was a deacon, my mother was a deaconess, my babysitter was a "Mother" in the church and did door-to-door witnessing, and my godmother was on the Mission Board. Their children were high school and college age, so I became the baby sister they took everywhere. And they told me things and showed me things that were really meant for their age. Basically, I was eight going on 18. Let's just say I was advanced beyond my years, my family had an in with the pastor, his wife, and their kids, and we all attended the same church. That was a good thing and a not-so-good thing. I was privy to way too much church information that a child just shouldn't be privy to.

Stay with me as I'm going somewhere. Just keep reading as if you're listening to me speak at one of the conferences you attend.

Alas, one spring night, the pastor's wife came to our house dressed only in her housecoat. She had a gun; not a good situation. (Sis, I can see your eyes getting wide right now as you ask, "How did you know it wasn't a good situation?") Because I was the one who answered the door that night. When she came into the house and immediately marched into the family room, it was clear she was angry and distraught. My junior high school-mind immediately went into Nancy Drew mode, and thought, *Oh, what's wrong with her?* Then as I looked at her a little more closely my mind said, "It's late, she has on a housecoat, and she's holding a gun." My mother saw my intense scrutiny of the pastor's wife's face and saw the wheels turning in my head, so she said to her, "Come on dear, let's go talk in the garage." As they brushed past me, my mother gave me that "Little girl if you don't go somewhere and sit down and stop trying to get in grown folks business" look. Her eyes told me, "You won't be hearing *this* conversation."

They talked in the garage. It seemed her husband had had an affair, and she was not happy about it. To put it mildly, she was livid. The other woman had miscarried the baby she was carrying, and Sister-Pastor-Wife had dropped her husband off at the hospital to deal with it. Then she came straight over to our house with the news.

I found all this out by using my *Mission Impossible* technique of putting a glass on the door and listening. Child, it worked! Anyway, my mother talked Sister-Pastor-Wife off the ledge, took the gun, and prayed for her. She also gave her some advice about staying or not staying. It was at that very moment that I promised myself I would never marry a preacher, let alone a pastor, and if my husband ever cheated on me, I was going to beat the hell out of him and the other woman, then take my kids and leave him. Period. End of story.

That Sister-Pastor-Wife didn't shoot the pastor-husband. She took him back, the church forgave him, and everyone moved on. Me at 12 thought that was the dumbest thing ever. And me at 45 still thought it was the stupidest thing ever. My mother (the deacon's wife) and my cousin (the pastor's wife) said these words to me, "Never say never, Laura, 'cause you don't know what you'd do in that situation." And those words, those same words came back to haunt me 34 years later.

Fast forward to my 1983 life. I was a freshman at Grambling State University and my cousin was now married to the pastor of my home church. Since I was home for the summer, I was the official babysitter for their two children. Once again, I was thrust into the adult world with adult problems. I had a front row seat into all of my cousin's challenges and the shenanigans of the church folks they pastored. What was going on? I always seemed to be at their house babysitting when interesting adult things happened. Again, I saw way too much. I saw women, I saw men, I saw children crying over the indiscretions in their marriage or those of their parents. I was getting tutored in Relationships 101: Marriage and Otherwise. The problems mostly related to marriage stuff, but some people were engaged, and some were dating. And some issues dealt with wayward children and how the parents handled the craziness. Nevertheless, somebody was always devastated. I went back to school and told myself once again I would never put up with any of that.

In 1992, I married my best friend of 22 years, who God told me was going to be a preacher. Now hear me, at that point, I was okay with that until June 8, 1996. That was the year my preacher-husband-friend became my pastor-preacher-husband-friend.

No!

Oh, my stars, I knew what that meant. My life as I knew it was over. Living in a fishbowl would commence, and so would the increase, influx, whatever word you want to use in reference to females, would begin. Now my husband would really be surrounded by women, and, as you know, that's mainly the make-up of most churches. I don't care what denomination we're talking about. All those females who "used-to-be-his-friends-females" would now be at the church as "church-females."

Ugh.

Big sigh.

Hmmmmm.

Yeah, the same ones I used to tell him were not really his friends, friends.

So, into ministry we went and here they came. Some even joined the church. And this is where I told him I was not going to be *that* wife. And I wasn't going to be *that* pastor's wife I had thought about being when I was 12. I reminded him of our discussion before we got married; you cheat on me, and we're done. Finito. No explanations and no discussions. I told him I would leave him and take our kids. My kids. There would be zero negotiations and no conversations. And that went well for almost 20 years. But in January of 2012, nah, really it was November 2010 but that's another story and another chapter, the fairytale marriage I thought I had, died.

Let me just say this—in 2012, the affair was physical, but in 2010 it was emotional as she pretended she needed pastoral help with her marriage since her husband had cheated on her. Girl, please. Let's stop right here and insert a scripture: "No temptation has overtaken you except such as is common to man; but God *is* faithful, who will not allow you to be tempted beyond what you are able, but with the temptation will also make the way of escape, that you may be able to bear *it,*" 1 Corinthians 10:13 (NKJV).

My dumb husband had fallen and did not get up. God showed me and told me. Weekly I would ask my husband, "Is there something you want to tell me?" And weekly he would say, "No." Then I would say, "Just tell me while we're still friends and I'm not angry." Pause. Breathe. "Is there something you want to share with me?" And again, he would say, "No."

Alrighty then.

This went on for 22 months; maybe even longer because I counted the times when they were just talking and texting before becoming physical. Then, I remembered the words the older women years before had said to me, "Never say never, Laura." And then I got angry.

I asked God why wouldn't my husband just come clean? So, he did—kind of. In November 2013 when he finally broke it off, I knew. I could tell. God even assured me it was over. But that wasn't enough for me. I was Jonah-ette. He didn't deserve to get off that easy. For me to have closure I wanted him to confess. I begged God to make him. Compel him. But He didn't. God simply said one thing to me, and it was disciplinary, "Don't insist on getting even; that's not for you to do. I'll do the judging. I'll take care of it," Romans 12:19.

Okay God. You handle it.

Now remember, I'm an only child. When I was growing up all I had was a big God and an old soul. God was my BFF. He talked to me just like I'm talking to you. We had conversations. And He always answered my requests, usually right away. Except for this time. This time there was silence.

Teachers don't answer students while students are taking a test.

Hence, God did not answer me.

Whatever.

I wanted an answer. I needed an answer. God is a good God, and a faithful Father. He knows what you can bear. God said to me, "Laura, I will answer you on

Wednesday." My heart knew God would keep His word and tell me in His time, but my mind was still wanting answers right then, so of course, I tried to get the answers my way. I called my husband in Louisiana. He was there because his father had passed, and he and his brothers had gone down earlier than their families to make the funeral arrangements. All of us were scheduled to go to Louisiana the week I wanted answers. So, I took matters into my own hands. You know how we try to hurry God. Manipulate God. Worry God for answers.

I started the fast Monday, August 25, 2014, and began reading Psalm 37. I figured if I fasted and prayed, God would respond to me. I also asked my children to join me in prayer and in the fast. They did. They hoped God would answer their mother. My kids had already discovered some dirt on their father and had already kept some things hidden from me trying to protect me. That Monday they prayed for God to answer me.

He did not.

Again, God said, "I will show you on Wednesday."

I woke up Tuesday morning and immediately asked God to reveal to me what really happened. God told me to keep reading Psalm 37; He wasn't going to answer me until Wednesday. Again, I wanted answers immediately, so I called my husband and said, "Is there something you want to tell me before I get to Louisiana? Before I put the kids on the plane today?" He stuck to his guns and replied, "No, Laura, because I haven't done anything!"

"I think you're lying!" I screamed back at him. Then ever so sweetly, calmly, and softly I continued. "I do not believe you! Just tell me you've been sleeping with her, and I'll leave it alone." I knew I'd have to play the role for just a little while longer.

Again, he insisted, "I didn't sleep with her, Laura!"

Yep. He was lying and I knew it. So, I said, "I don't believe you and God is going to show it to me, so you might as well confess!" Tony just sighed into the phone. But I knew he was trying to buy time. I told God, "I know he's lying and You're gonna show me."

After I hung up the phone, the kids and I headed off to the airport. I put three of my four kids onto an American Airlines flight to Louisiana with my sister-in-law. I was a complete wreck. My oldest son and I said our goodbyes and amidst tears, told them we'd see them Friday. My two daughters and youngest son didn't want to leave Mom crazy like that, but they had to leave. They told their brother to take care of me. He was the quarterback for his football team, and the first game was that Thursday, so he and I stayed back. God knew what He was doing.

Although I hated to see the kids go, I knew I could have some alone time with God while my son was at football practice. During that time, I tried to figure out if I was right about my husband and what I believed he did. I whined to God and repeatedly called and sent texts to my husband. I was determined to make him confess. And each time he was adamant nothing had gone on and he was completely innocent. I knew he wasn't innocent. Remember, I've been his friend since we were five years old. He knew I knew he was lying. So, I went back to God, and cried, "Why won't You tell me?" Silence.

I couldn't eat. I couldn't sleep, and I lost a lot of

weight during those two days. Why is that so important for you to know? For me weight is an issue. But for the record, when I'm bored, happy, or content, I eat. When I'm angry or sad, I drop pounds like nothing. But I digress.

After all the no sleeping, the no eating, and the losing of a lot of weight, I still didn't have a definitive answer. But I did have Psalm 37. "Do not fret because of evildoers, nor be envious of the workers of iniquity. For they shall soon be cut down like the grass and wither as the green herb. Trust in the Lord, and do good; Dwell in the land, and feed on His faithfulness. Delight yourself also in the Lord, and He shall give you the desires of your heart" Psalm 37:1-4 NKJV.

I found comfort in that. God was going to vindicate me. I'm not going to tell you I didn't act up when my husband called me later that Tuesday night. But I will tell you once again God had no words for me.

None.

But on Wednesday, August 27, 2014, I knew my God would do as He promised. He told me I'd know everything that day. And I woke up with feelings of both expectancy and dread. This would be the day He would reveal all the answers I needed. Notice I said, "the answers I needed." Remember that.

God didn't answer me until I had dropped my son off at mid-morning football practice. When I got back to the house I jumped on the scale and to my delight I had lost 13 pounds! I was ecstatic with the weight loss, giddy almost, but hated the reason I had gotten there. God quietly said, "Today is the day. Today I will show you everything you've asked Me." The house was completely silent. Still. There wasn't a child, a church member, or a neighbor who stopped by. It was just me and Jesus. He said, "Read Psalm 37 again, but this time..." and there it was. Right in front of my face. Verse seven, "Rest in the Lord, and wait patiently for him; fret not thyself because of him who prospereth in his way, because of the man who bringeth wicked devices to pass."

Devices! His computer! That's it! The evil device: the baby laptop that had been sitting in our room for months while he was away taking care of his dying father. It had been there the entire time with every shred of evidence I thought I needed. I literally had every piece of evidence I needed to leave him. And that's exactly what I had planned to do: leave his King James Version donkey behind. I found everything. Everything.

And then the computer died.

Completely shut off.

And then God spoke to me. It was a still, quiet voice. He told me to call Tony; don't yell, and don't scream.

Wait. Are you serious? God are You serious?

Yes. Yes, I'm serious.

Tell him you love him. Tell him you are not going to leave him or take the kids. Tell him that you are not going to divorce him. Say it just like that. Calmly. Quietly.

Absolutely not.

I. Will. Not.

I am not going to do that.

I won't.

Then I went back to the laptop, and it wouldn't power up. God whispered, "You've seen enough. It's not going to come back on."

I plugged it up instead. *The battery must've died*, I thought to myself.

God said, "No, it's not the battery or the power. It's not coming back on. You've seen enough."

I plugged that laptop into every socket upstairs. I checked the breaker to see if the electricity was off. It was not. His third and final time God said to me, "It's not coming back on. It's not going to power up. You've seen enough. Now call Tony and tell him what I told you to say."

I was livid. No, I was enraged! I had no nice words. I stomped and screamed all through the house. I cussed out Tony in my mind, and I said some not so nice words to God.

He listened. He let me cry. He let me yell. He let me cry some more.

And then I called him. I called Tony. Shame washed over me. I remembered all the women I had ever counseled whose husbands had cheated on them. How would I be able to face them? What could I say? I told every one of them to leave their husbands. Well, not all of them. Two of the husbands I genuinely loved, so I gave them a pass. Ain't that like us? People we like who we catch in sin, it's ok and we forgive them without issue. But all the other husbands who I didn't like so much, I'm ashamed to say, I had told these wives to leave those no-good-you-fill-in-the-blanks.

Even now, the judgmental me remembers what I said, and I cringe. I remember how relieved my husband's voice was when I said I wasn't going to leave him, take the kids, or divorce him. I did, however, roll my eyes. I couldn't believe I still loved him.

God said, "Forgive him."

My response was, "Yeah, sure."

I cried out in my empty house, "How will I ever face those women I told to leave their husbands? What can I possibly say? And You want me to do WHAT?!?!"

So, God said a few things to me. One was, "You made Tony an idol. You put him on a pedestal, and I clearly said you shall have no other gods before me, "therefore, my beloved, flee from idolatry" Exodus 20:3 and 1 Corinthians 10:14.

"God," I responded, "Tony was my friend. I saw him do all this kind of stuff to other women. I never thought he'd do this to me."

God gently said, "You looked to him instead of me."

Wow. I had to repent and apologize to God. He asked me if I trusted Him, and I did, so He gave me peace with by reminding me of the verse that says that I could "do all things through Christ who strengthens me" Philippians 4:13 NKJV. In my weakness, is when God made me strong. And I really needed strength. I had to talk to myself many a day about staying. Did I want to be obedient to God, or disobedient? Right here, insert one big giant sigh.

For a long time, I was angry and felt stupid for taking my husband back. Even today, I've been triggered, but God reminded me in Psalm 30:5, "For his anger endureth but a moment; in his favour is life: weeping may endure for a night, but joy cometh in the morning." This scripture got me through many nights and awful mornings. I would also cling to the verse that says, "Trust in the Lord with all thine heart; and lean not unto thine own understanding. In all thy ways acknowledge him, and he shall direct thy paths" Proverbs 3:5-6 NKJV. I leaned on and repeated that scripture over and over again during the many months and years of healing and restoration. I would remind myself that God loved me and forgave me. He forgave me for all the wrong I did to Him.

But I never imagined I'd find my joy, or the love I thought I lost for my husband and my marriage. Because I did lose it for a while. Don't let anyone tell you that you don't lose a part of yourself, your heart, or the love you thought you had for the spouse that betrayed you. And you're angry.

I was mad.

I was so mad *at* God.

I was mad *with* God.

I was mad *at* myself. Really mad.

I was mad with the church people who knew.

I was mad with the cousins who, to me, took his side.

I was mad with my mom.

I was mad because they all loved and believed in Tony, and they all forgave him. "He made a mistake," they would say, and that would infuriate me. I could barely sit and listen to my husband preach weekly. He would literally weave David into all his sermons, not even realizing he was preaching about our situation.

In this season, God knew what He was doing, even if I was questioning His sovereignty. At this time, we had merged with another church and the pastor preached about David during the installation/appreciation service, and I was sitting there like, "Really God? Is this really happening?" And at the end of the service when it was time for each of us to give remarks, the people (our church and the visiting churches) said I got up there and said I wasn't leaving him and that I still loved him. Y'all to this day I don't remember saying that.

My girlfriend called and asked me that Sunday night and then asked me again in person that Monday at lunch, "Girl, why did you say you still loved him, and you were going to stay with him? Why did you say that you weren't going to leave him? Did you mean to say that?" I told her I didn't even remember that night. I remember crying. I remember yelling at God. I remember not wanting to get dressed and to go to the installation. But, even to this day, I don't remember saying any of that.

What I can say is, "But God."

How have I found my joy again? Well, if I'm honest, on some days I haven't. On other days, the power of the Holy Spirit is so strong that He leads me to peace and contentment. I won't lie, and I'll be brutally transparent. Some days are a struggle. Anger or resentment or bitterness will rear their ugly heads, and I will shut down. Won't say a word. Won't pray. Won't read my Bible. Will just sit and whine and complain to God.

And some days, I won't. I won't even part my lips. I won't say anything to God, and I won't say anything *at all* to Tony. I used to go days with zero words and zero love for Tony Simon. But thank God those days are gone.

I will say this. God's ways are not our ways. God can handle your problems far better than you ever can. And in another book, I'll tell you about the time God handled my husband in a way I never would have.

Wow, what I can say? And wow, you can't outdo God when it comes to dishing out punishment.

So, Sis, the feelings of shame I had before when telling my story are gone. However, let me share this; writing this was a serious struggle for me. I had to address the unforgiveness I was still harboring and nursing in my heart. I still think this part of my story is unfair. I still think God let my husband off easy. I even hate the fact I still want to beat up the other woman. Yep. I said it out loud. I am so not proud of that. I am also not proud of the fact that my mother and anybody else who knows our story feels for Tony. I really hate that, too. I can play the Victim Card quite nicely. And then I feel guilty when I start looking at 1 Thessalonians 5:14-15. This is the hardest thing I have ever had to do. We must die to ourselves daily. We must take up our own cross and carry it. I don't like this cross. And some days I'm mad about carrying this cross even though God has said He would carry it for me. His burden is light, but I'm just not ready to let Him have it. That's real.

My husband is still struggling with when to share his perspective. He feels it needs to be told, but it's one thing to share in a conference or counseling environment, and quite another to share on paper. That's forever. Pray for us both on that.

We both realize this had to happen. It changed both of us. It really changed me. I was open and honest before, but this is such a humbling thing. These kinds of humbling situations make you re-evaluate your relationship with God, with your spouse, and with others. You examine all your relationships. And you make sure your new relationships and your old ones are ordained by God, so you won't have to endure stuff like this again. Our marriage is stronger. It's healthier, and we communicate more and often. We have talked openly to couples about the dangers of adultery and hidden sin; how they have the potential to destroy lives; the lives of your children; your extended family; your church; and your influence.

Adultery and hidden sin can destroy *you*.

The enemy so wanted to silence my witness. He still does. And he still tries. That's why I said this whole thing is a struggle. I don't want to help the enemy do his job, but sometimes I do. The shame of people finding out at first held me hostage. But when I started sharing my hurt and pain, other women found courage to share their hard stories. Look, I'm not saying I'm perfect, or I have perfect advice, but I am telling you God can change the situation. *Any* situation.

Reflection Corner

After reading these passages, what are your thoughts?

Colossians 3:13 NKJV "...bearing with one another, and forgiving one another, if anyone has a complaint against another; even as Christ forgave you, so you also must do."

Colossians 3:13 MSG "...Be even tempered, content with second place, quick to forgive an offense. Forgive as quickly and completely as the Master forgave you."

_____

_____

_____

_____

_____

_____
_____
_____
_____
_____

_____.
Romans 12:9-21 (MSG) - After reading this passage, what are your thoughts?

_____
_____
_____
_____
_____
_____
_____
_____
_____
_____
_____
_____
_____
_____

_____What words of advice or would you give to someone in this type of situation?

_____
_____
_____
_____
_____
_____

Now meditate on Galatians 6:1-5 MSG and answer the above question again. Verses 1-3 says, "Live creatively, friends. If someone falls into sin, forgivingly restore him, saving your critical comments for yourself. You might be needing forgiveness before the day's out. Stoop down and reach out to those who are oppressed. Share their burdens, and so complete Christ's law. If you think you are too good for that, you are badly deceived." And 4-5 says, "Make a careful exploration of who you are and the work you have been given, and then sink yourself into that. Don't be impressed with yourself. Don't compare yourself with others. Each of you must take responsibility for doing the creative best you can with your own life."

Wow. That part. The Bible just said it for me, to me, for you, to you, for us, to us. Wowzers.

Those verses humbled and still humble me. Check yourself before you wreck yourself.

Reflections, Questions, Things to Ponder

So, what, if anything changed in you about this type of situation? Do you have a different perspective or a different view on my story? What do you think you would've done? What wisdom would you have shared with me? Write about it and send it to me. I'd love to hear your take.

_____
_____
_____
_____
_____
_____
_____
_____
_____
_____
_____
_____
_____
_____
_____.

What's your hard story? Share it with someone who may need to hear how God brought you through and helped you navigate the difficult situation.

PRAYER

Father,

In Jesus Name, help me to truly live 1 Thessalonians 5:14-15 and see the best in my husband, and see the best in people. Remind me God to forgive others as you have so graciously and continuously forgiven me. Help me, Oh God, to remember I can also so easily be overtaken in a fault, that I am not immune to temptation, and that I've fallen short many times. And when I don't want to forgive, Father, give me the strength to forgive, and forgive again. God, help me to not only see the best in people, but to make sure that I bring out the best in them. In Jesus Name. Amen.

Author Biography

Laura Simon is a pastor's wife, mother, mentor, speaker, award-winning author, and Sister-Girlfriend who's passionate about pastor's wives, millennials, and women in ministry. A graduate of Grambling State University and National University, this girl is a former elementary school teacher, Allstate Claims Rep and Underwriter, Marriott Travel CSR, First American UCC Specialist, Administrative Assistant at Cal State Fullerton, and now Administrative Assistant in Everything to Pastor Sagel Anthony Simon, Sr, whom she affectionately calls "Tony Simon". This imperfectly imperfect person did a whole lot of searching before finally finding her perfect purpose: working with women leaders, helping them by sharing her sometimes brutally honest, but oh so transparent stories about living an authentic life in the ministry fishbowl. Lady Laura is most loved because of her unique ability to bridge the gap between the fiction and reality of her pastor-wife-life. This California-Only-Child-Native raised by Louisiana-Several-Sibling-Parents lives in Santa Ana, California with her PastorMan-Hubby, four children, Kennedy, twins Sagel II and Sydni, and not-so-baby-boy Jonathan. Covenant City Fellowship is where they lead.